So You Want to Move to Costa Rica?

My Quest for the Ultimate Tropical Paradise

By Frederic Patenaude

About the Author

Frederic Patenaude

Frederic Patenaude has been working in the natural health movement since 1998. He is the author of seven books, including *The Raw Secrets*, and his articles are read by tens of thousands of people every week.

Frederic spends his time in his home country of Canada and part of the year in a tropical location like Costa Rica or Thailand.

Other books & courses from or published by Frederic:

For a complete list of available books and products, and free subscription to Fred's e-mail tips on making a living doing what you love, go to: **www.dowhatyoulove.com**

This book is dedicated to the wonderful people of Costa Rica.

Acknowledgements

This book only could have been written after extensive experience living and visiting Costa Rica and other countries around the world. In my travels, so many people have contributed to my understanding of the issues raised in this book. I would like to thank Jacqui Monacell, of *yourcostaricacontact.com*, who so generously helped me throughout my various adventures in the country; thanks to Lic. Bernardo Vanderlaat, who helped me gain a better understanding of Costa Rican law; thanks to Eric Rivkin of vivalaraw.org, for his wonderful projects and his invaluable help; thanks to the editors of Tico Times and A.M. Costa Rica for their uncensored news reporting on what really goes on in the country; thanks to all the good friends I met on my various trips to Costa Rica; thanks to the people of Costa Rica, for their generous spirit; thanks to Kazzrie, my first host in Costa Rica, who became an invaluable contact; thanks to Aaron M. Dyer, Raina Vargas, Hugo Monge, Christopher Howard, Michael Greenward, and Steve Fisk.

Table of Contents

Things I Hate About the Winter, or How I Decided to Move to the Tropics

The famous French language poet Gilles Vignault wrote of Quebec, "My country is not a country, it's winter" (*Mon pays c'est pas un pays, c'est l'hiver*). Although it doesn't translate that well from French, I still think it summarizes well the love/hate relationship many Northerners have with winter.

On the one hand, the winter defines who we are. On the other hand, we despise the hardships of the cold season. Other satirical comments have been made about the winter in Canada and the Northern States, such as "We have two seasons in Canada, cold and not as cold."

I was born and raised in Montreal, Canada, and I struggled with the harsh winters there every year of my life. Finally, I started to spend my winters in warmer climates, and my life started to improve. I did my research, I visited and spent time in a variety of tropical paradises around the world, I even purchased a retreat center in Costa Rica (which I eventually did not keep). This book contains a distillation of the results of my research and experience. I give you specific details about a variety of tropical destinations and how to choose the right one for you. If you choose Costa Rica, as I did, you'll even find specific contact information to help get you started there.

However, after all that effort, I didn't make the permanent move to paradise. These days, I live in Canada in the warmer months, and relocate to Costa Rica or other tropical places to escape some of the northern winter.

If you're interested in moving to a tropical paradise, but are unsure whether you'd fit in with the different culture there, my experiences will help you to make up your mind.

I was told that the best way to get through the winter is to embrace it. Instead of cursing the weather, make the best of it. Go out and enjoy some winter sports! Ski! Put on some warm clothes and go take a walk when it's sunny outside, even if it's below freezing. That all sounds good, but even with this advice, I still hated the winter.

I did not care for skiing or other winter sports. I much preferred feeling the wind on my skin as I rode my bike or ran outside, with sunshine on my face, rather than sweating uncomfortably in a giant insulated winter coat, while risking frostbite to every exposed part of my body. Getting in and out of the house becomes a big endeavor in winter, requiring a lot of preparation, rather than something simple and enjoyable. Even with a well-intentioned plan, like scheduling a 45-minute walk every morning, the power of the elements can dampen the firmest commitment.

There were times when the weather was so cold, I remained literally locked in my house for almost a week at a time. Even going out to the gym wasn't something I was willing to do.

Other random winter annoyances include:

- Being cold in the morning when getting out of bed
- Salt on the streets corroding everything
- Shoveling snow
- Snow melting into slush and brown from the dirt, staining and wetting everything

2

- Scarf smell! The nasty phenomenon that happens when you breathe your own snot smell from having to wear a scarf over your nose and mouth.

- Having to get into a freezing cold car that never actually starts to warm up until you're about to reach your destination

- Cold feet and toes!

- Snow gets in the way of everything!

- Sunrise at 8:30 a.m. and sunset at 4:00 p.m.

- Chapped lips because of indoor heating

- The time it takes to get dressed just to go outside for any reason!

- Ice, and the dangers it brings

- Christmas songs playing in early November with no respite until late in December

Health Aspects of Living in the North

I found that although it was possible to stay healthy in the North, and to continue eating a mostly raw food diet (which kept me healthy), the winter made it much more difficult to stay healthy and in shape.

First, there's the problem of temperature. Setting the thermostat between 65 and 68 degrees (18-20 Celsius) is supposed to be healthy, but it feels too cold. Try boosting the temperature above that, and you start feeling the negative effects of artificial heating: dry skin, respiratory problems and discomfort.

So my sad solution was to keep the temperature low, but wear extra layers in the house. I always kept the bathroom steaming hot, as I hated entering a cold bathroom to take a shower on a Monday morning.

The problems of the cold weather were exacerbated by eating cold foods, such as fresh fruit from the fridge. I had to be particularly careful to avoid all cold drinks and fruits, otherwise I would get the shivers.

3

Sometimes, after eating a big smoothie with fruits straight from the fridge, I would feel so cold that I had to take a hot bath to feel better.

As soon as the weather started getting cold, I would lose my motivation to exercise outside, which is my favorite type of exercise. So I had to find other types of exercises that could be done inside, such as rebounding or going to the gym.

The shorter days with less sunshine meant little vitamin D for the entire winter, which could be hard for the body to bear without supplementation.

I did find, however, that despite the difficulties of eating raw in the North, the health advantages of eating this way far outweighed the negatives. Most of my friends and relatives got seriously sick at least once every winter, and would often complain of stuffed noses or colds, while I remained healthy and cold-free the entire winter. My mood was dramatically improved by the natural "sunshine" I got from the fruits and vegetables I was eating, and the exercise routine I tried to maintain.

Over the years I spent eating raw in Canada, I even came up with a series of recipes and tips for following a raw food diet in the North, called the **Raw Winter Recipe Guide**.

However, there is no doubt that staying fit and healthy is dramatically easier in a warmer climate, unless you are a winter sports freak.

The Winter Amnesia

Every winter, I tried to spend at least a few weeks in a warmer climate. From 2000-2003, I was in California in the winter. In 2004, I spent one month in Brazil. In 2005, I spent three months in Costa Rica. In 2006, I went to Bali and French Polynesia. In 2007, I spent five months in Costa Rica. Every year, I was avoiding more and more of the winter… but part of me was still attached to living in the North with its four seasons. Call it nostalgia?

I have a different name for it. I call it *winter amnesia.*

I came up with this concept with a friend of mine back in 2003. At the time, I had noticed something strange. I would go through an entire winter of hardship, cold and snow, and when spring and summer came, I'd start thinking that living in Canada wasn't so bad after all.

I would think to myself: "Maybe I don't have to move anywhere warm after all. It's not so bad."

I would completely forget how horrible the winter was… and that's how I realized I had winter amnesia, a common psychological affliction among Northerners, who purposely forget how bad winters are, in order to stay in their comfort zone and avoid any radical move!

So I would set myself up for another cold winter, without making the necessary move to a warmer climate.

It got to the point that I actually asked my friend to send me an email in November of that year. The email I asked him to send me read something like this:

Dear Frederic,

I know that by now you've come out of a very enjoyable summer in Canada, and you have completely forgotten how bad last winter was. This letter is to remind you: get out of there before it's too late! The winter sucks! Your friend,

Yourself

Frederic

Of course, this "winter amnesia" concept was just a joke, but there was some truth behind it. Unless I planned for it in advance, there was no way I was going to fulfill my dream of living in a warmer climate.

Fast forward to the present day: I'm now living in Vancouver, which experiences very mild winters, and I spend at least 1-2 months of the year in the tropics. I have no intention of experiencing another northern winter again for any reason!

When I lived in Montreal, I would sometimes wait until January 10th to go on my annual winter trip, and I regretted it terribly.

The months of November and December in Montreal were truly horrible, so I swore to myself that I would never stay for another winter again.

Call me a winter wussy, but I came to the conclusion that the months of November through April were completely out of the question (at least in Quebec). I HAD to be in a warm climate during that time. May isn't so bad, because there's the promise of summer. June is okay. July and August are the only great months. September is also good because of the sunny weather, harvest time and beautiful trees dropping leaves. October is already off-limits. It's tolerable, but not enjoyable. I'd rather be heading somewhere else!

I've spent many winters in Costa Rica. For many years, I kept my apartment year-round in Canada, and spent several months in Costa Rica during the winter. In 2009, my ex-wife and I decided to get rid of most of our possessions in Canada to establish a more permanent base in Costa Rica.

We stayed there for six months, and then traveled the world for one year. After that, we relocated to Vancouver, BC, and still spend a few months of the winter in the tropics.

How to Escape the Winter

Although I didn't like winter in the first place, as I spent more and more time in sunny and tropical countries, I started disliking it even more.

At first, what I needed was at least a few weeks away from the cold every winter. Then, I increased that amount to a month or two. At some point, it became clear that I wanted to avoid the months of January, February and March completely. Then I realized that December also sucked, and so did April. So I made it a rule I would never come back to Canada before May. But November is also pretty bad, so last year I decided to leave before the end of October.

At some point, I started avoiding winter completely. And let me tell you, I was not missing it one bit!

My advice if you're dreaming about doing this is to start slowly. Take trips, a little bit at a time like I did, rather than deciding to move somewhere completely like many people do (and often regret).

Research certain countries, and then take a "field trip" to investigate what it would be like to live there.

If you like what you see, consider staying for a longer period.

It's not that hard to do if you work for yourself. The trickiest part is finding a place that you can rent for a few months only, to keep your costs down.

But if you spend the winter in a place like Costa Rica, Panama or Thailand, you can save, even if you keep your apartment and house back home!

Because the cost of living is much lower in these countries, even though you might spend extra on a plane ticket and rent, you'll save in other areas, such as food and entertainment — so in the end, it often balances out, and your total expenses stay the same.

The Cost of Living in a Tropical Paradise

It seems that money is the most important factor holding people back from trying out living abroad, when in fact it shouldn't be such a big issue if you find the right place to go and set up your life accordingly.

"Moving to a tropical paradise" either implies a long-term move where you live in your new home year round, or a seasonal arrangement, where you stay in the tropical paradise for one to six months a year.

In both cases, it's possible to do this while increasing your overall standard of living and decreasing your overall yearly expenses.

Personally, I've come to prefer the seasonal setup, where I typically spend one to three months a year in a tropical paradise, and the rest of the year in my home country of Canada or travelling somewhere else.

This allows me to enjoy the best of both worlds. And because I'm establishing a "cradle" overseas, I always have the option to spend more time in "Paradise" in the future.

I suggest that you do the same at first. Don't plan an unrealistic and sudden move.

But if you're serious about increasing your quality of life and moving to a tropical paradise — full-time or part-time — soon or in the near future — then you need to start taking some steps to making that dream a reality.

I know some people who claim to have visited 30 or 50+ countries. In most cases, they have only spent a few days in those countries, and have visited them as tourists, staying in popular tourist areas. That's not an adequate basis for this type of decision.

I haven't just toured the world superficially: I've gotten to know several tropical places *intimately*.

When I visited Brazil for over a month, I rarely stayed in a hotel. I prepared myself for this trip by studying Portuguese for two years! During the trip, I stayed with Brazilian friends and spoke Portuguese. I got to know the country much better than most people could in the same amount of time.

I've visited Spain several times, and have some dear friends who live there. I'm not an expert on Spain, but I have a pretty good idea of the country.

I lived in London for many months, and I studied in Germany at the Goethe Institute when I was doing my language studies.

The "tropical" country I know best is Costa Rica, but I have also spent a significant amount of time in Bali, Hawaii, and the South Pacific.

I've lived in the United States for 3 years, and have visited many times since then. Being from the French part of Canada (and having visited most Canadian provinces), I think I have a pretty good perspective on the world as a whole.

I also made a complete move to Costa Rica back in 2006, but decided later that I preferred living most of the year in Canada and some months in places like Costa Rica. So I'm well aware of the issues related to completely relocating to a new country.

So, let's start with the cost of living.

Cost of Living in Paradise

Let's start by saying that there is no standard "cost of living" for a given country. In most countries nowadays, you can spend as much as you want and live in total luxury, and in many countries you can live decently on a rock-bottom budget.

For example, in Costa Rica you can find rents for luxury condos that go as high as $2000 per week, and at the budget level you can find a cheap apartment in the city for maybe $200 per month.

But I know this is not going to answer your question, so let's start with food.

Let's start with the cost of fruits and vegetables.

Here's a few things I bought in 2011 in Costa Rica, with the prices in US dollars according to the latest exchange rate:

- 6 small avocados, Hass variety: $2, or about 35 cents per avocado
- 1 medium-sized watermelon: $6
- 1 small box of bananas containing about 36 bananas: $2.72 (or 7 cents per banana)
- 3 deliciously plant-ripened pineapples: $3 or about $1 per pineapple

To give you a comparison, in Montreal we used to get avocados 2 for a dollar. Now they rarely sell below $1.50. Often you'll see them for $1.99 or more.

The avocados I bought were not huge, but they were tasty.

Pineapples of the same size cost about $4.99 in Canada. Sometimes they sell for $5.99 or more.

Watermelon is not the cheapest fruit in Costa Rica, but a similar watermelon back home would cost me 2 or 3 times the price.

Let me give you some more Costa Rica prices:

- A large 2 liter bottle of spring water is $1.50
- A typical cooked lunch at a local restaurant is less than $3.50
- You can buy an entire cluster of bananas (that's a LOT of bananas) for less than $6
- Taxi fares are still very cheap. I get a cab ride back to my place from the farmers' market (maybe a 20-minute walk) for about $2.50.
- You can rent a taxi for an entire day for about $60-70 (that means the taxi and driver are available to you all day to take you anywhere you like).
- The minimum charge on my cellphone is $8 per month.
- Internet is priced about the same or higher than in the US.
- Quality appliances are much more expensive than they are in the US or Canada, but local, cheap brands are about the same price.
- Property taxes are extremely cheap by American standards. For example, a huge property and farm might pay only $300 per year for property taxes.
- You can hire a maid full-time for about $350 per month.

Some things are more expensive:

- Because of import taxes, buying a car is more expensive (about 30 to 40% more), so it's best to buy a used car or live somewhere where you don't need one, and use cabs or rent a car when needed.
- Clothes are more expensive, if you want designer labels.
- Other items such as electronics, computers, cameras and small appliances are more expensive.

Costa Rica is not the cheapest country in the world. A lot of the things you buy will cost about the same as you pay back home. A few will cost more. And many will cost a lot less.

People say that on average the cost of living is about 30% lower than in the United States, and maybe 50% lower than Canada.

Of course, it also depends where YOU live. If you live in Atlanta, Georgia, you are already accustomed to a low cost of living. But if you live in San Francisco, you will see a big difference.

A lot of people are looking for a place that is affluent and safe, but has absolutely rock bottom prices.

According to my experience, this place does not exist.

But you can find very affordable living in a very stable, friendly, welcoming and affluent country such as Costa Rica.

If you're looking for really cheap living, with welcoming people and a safe environment, but are okay with seeing some poverty around you, then I recommend you check out South East Asia.

I've visited many countries in the area, such as Indonesia, Thailand, and the Philippines.

Let's compare Thailand with Costa Rica, for example:

- A cooked meal from a street vendor is about $1, compared to $3.50 in Costa Rica
- Mangoes are about 30 cents a pound or less. In Costa Rica you can find them for 50 cents a pound (but a lot less during the height of the mango season)
- Avocados are 12 cents each, compared to 30 cents or more in Costa Rica
- Taxis are even CHEAPER in Asia

Rent

Now let's talk about rent, in Costa Rica and elsewhere.

Most people suffer from "real estate fever" as soon as they land in a tropical country. I think it's worse than any other tropical disease!

They've been in this new country for less than a week, and they are already considering buying property. They've fallen in love with the place, and they're ready to buy.

This is a big no-no…

Of course, the real estate agents will tell you that you're missing out if you don't buy RIGHT NOW! And that people who bought only one year ago are getting rich from appreciation.

But what they don't tell you is that all of these "gains" are unrealized because nobody has sold their place.

They bought it for $100,000. Now it's "worth" $150,000. But of course no one is there to buy it.

Right now, with the recession, it's a buyer's market. But according to most predictions, it will become an even better buyer's market if you wait.

Personally, I don't see the point in buying a house in a foreign country until you've decided that you're absolutely positive it's where you want to live for a long time, either full time or as a second residence.

I value my freedom too much to want to make that decision now. I like the flexibility to be able to move whenever I want.

Remember: it's very easy to BUY, but not always so easy to SELL!

I know because I have hands-on experience buying property in Costa Rica, but having the hardest time selling it.

So, renting is what makes the most sense at first, and most experts suggest renting for at least 6 months in one area before thinking about buying anything.

Remember: there are always good deals to be found!

Let's take the case of Costa Rica.

Even though Costa Rica is a relatively small country, it's still full of completely different sub-climates and environments.

A lot of people fantasize about living on the beach. But you won't know what it's like until you *live* there.

Personally, I wouldn't want to live on the beach. It's too hot for my taste, and just not my preference in general. I prefer some elevation, with cool refreshing wind.

I love to *go* to the beach, but not live *on* the beach.

So I think you need time to explore living in different areas before finding the place that you really like, where you want to settle.

Now, let's get back to the rent:

When I was single, I paid $325 per month for a 1-bedroom apartment on a 6-month lease. If I had wanted, I could have paid month by month for $375.

The apartment was fully furnished. It had a fridge, appliances, cable-TV included (which was great for watching movies and following news at home), a small kitchen, and a main living room. In the living room (which was separated from the kitchen by a breakfast bar), I had my "office" setup, with a desk and a printer/scanner, and my Internet connection.

There was a balcony with a hammock, and a beautiful view of the mountains and the city where I lived.

I had banana plants growing right in my backyard.

It also had air conditioning, but I found I rarely wanted to use it. The temperature was almost perfect–about 82 degrees during the day, dropping to 64 at night. There was always a cool, refreshing breeze.

Now… where could *you* find a place like this?

The most common place people look is **Craigslist**.

Sometimes you'll find great deals on Craigslist, but more often than not, these "deals" are targeted toward foreigners.

The really great places are not advertised on Craigslist. You'll find them through local contacts, and through local real estate agents. On the other hand, in my experience Craigslist is a great place to find apartments for short-term stays.

My Last Long Term Stay in Costa Rica

I spent 4 winters in Costa Rica as a single guy. In 2009, I met my ex-wife, and we decided to try living in Costa Rica for six months, with the possibility of relocating there full time.

When we first got to Costa Rica, we looked for a place to stay. In the pages that follow, I will review all the possible spots in Costa Rica and where to go for the best value.

We eventually settled near the town of Quepos, close to the beautiful National Park Manuel Antonio.

We rented an apartment at the Villas Tranquilas (**http://www. villastranquilas.com/**), that we found on Craigslist. Our rent was around $1200 a month. Although that may seem high, the place was a two-story, two bedroom house, with access to the resort pool. A similar place in Miami, Florida, would probably rent for at least $3000 a month, and it would be hard to get it on a six-month lease, which was easy in Costa Rica.

You'll End Up Spending Less!

If you think money is an issue, think again! If you live frugally, it's possible to lower your total expenses by spending 5 months of the year in Costa Rica.

In Quebec, I had an apartment. I paid around $900 per month for rent.

So what did I do with that place when I was gone?

Nothing.

I just locked the door, and left.

I had some friends and family who stopped by once in a while and checked to make sure everything was okay.

I didn't sublet it or rent it when I was gone.

So how come it cost me LESS?

Here's where I saved:

- My food costs dropped dramatically when I was in a tropical paradise. Because I eat lots of fruits and vegetables, I spend a lot of money on groceries in Canada. About $600 per month on average (just for myself). In Costa Rica, this drops to $200-300, so I save $300-400 per month right there.
- I cancelled my car insurance while I was gone, and saved $115 per month.
- I also cancelled my car licenses when I was away, and saved some money there.
- I had a much lower heating bill than if I stayed at home. If I stayed

at home, I would spend $100 per month (or more) on heating. My bill dropped to maybe $20 per month just to maintain a decent temperature and make sure things didn't freeze!

- I changed my phone plan to the cheapest one available during that time away.
- I cancelled Internet while I was away, and reactivated it when I came back.

So these are some of the ways I save hundreds of dollars. This paid for my apartment in Costa Rica, right off the bat.

But I haven't talked about one important reduction in cost of living: the *Pura Vida* life!

The Costa Ricans have a saying, "Pura Vida" — pure life — which they use in almost every situation.

What I've found is that when I'm in the "spending" culture of North America, I'm naturally inclined to spend more.

There are things to do, things to buy, and most everything costs more.

I spend money renting DVDs (or streaming movies on Netflix or iTunes), buying the latest electronic gadgets, and so on and so forth.

In Costa Rica, my big fun is to go to swim under waterfalls, go for a hike, go to the beach. These don't cost anything.

And it's not that I don't enjoy life there!

I do spend for extras such as going scuba diving, renting a car to explore a new area of the country, and even flying to Panama for a short trip, to go snorkeling on some island.

It's just that the culture is not forcing you to *Buy! Buy! Buy!*

I do spend money on eBooks and keep up with my education while I'm there. I just stop spending money on things that I don't really need.

Earning Money While in Paradise

Everybody wants to know how they can earn money in Paradise. They want to know the rules for immigration and working in the new country.

You have two options for making money in Paradise:

1. Make your money remotely through business or activities based back in Canada, Europe, the USA, or wherever you normally live, and simply draw some income to pay for your expenses here.

2. Work in the country.

I personally feel the first option is best for most people.

Basically, anything that can be done for money with a computer and an Internet connection can be done anywhere in the world!

You'll generate income, pay your taxes in your home country just like you would normally, and withdraw some cash through the ATM machine to pay for your lifestyle in paradise.

Here are some possibilities:

*   Sell eBooks online, or generate income through an online business
*   Sell your services through websites such as www.elance.com, for proof-reading, editing, transcription work, online customer service, web design, and things of that nature.
*   Work as a remote travel agent (this work can be done with a computer)
*   Work as a travel writer
*   Become a blogger and find a way to generate income from your website
*   And more!

If you want a true vacation, then you can work seasonally back home, and find a way to take off one to six months a year, and live off your savings during that time. I know plenty of people who do that.

If you want to work IN the country, by setting up your own business, bed and breakfast, or retail store, here's one thing most people don't realize:

You can start a business in Costa Rica on a tourist visa.

In Costa Rica, it's perfectly legal to arrive on a tourist visa, start your own company, and open a retail store or bed and breakfast, hire employees and generate income while you're here.

The only thing you can't do is hire other foreigners or hire yourself as an employee of your own company. But you can certainly own and manage the company... all of it on a tourist visa!

Then the tricky thing is you have to leave the country every 90 days to renew your visa. But I find that's a great time to go to Panama or another place for a short trip.

Of course, there are plenty of residency options... but in my opinion you don't need to worry about that until you're absolutely positive you want to live there permanently.

Other countries have different rules, so make sure you are fully informed before starting a business in any country.

Now that I've shown you how affordable it can be to live in paradise at least part of the year, you've got one of the main obstacles out of the way!

A Realistic Approach to Cost of Living in Costa Rica

There's no doubt that Costa Rica is a cheaper place to live than any first-world nation. However, a lot of the savings come from the fact that Costa Rica is still a developing country.

It may not be a "third-world" country (you won't see abject poverty here like you do in Mexico or Honduras), but it is certainly not a first world one either. "Second world" would probably be the best description, but that doesn't mean much!

The average Costa Rican (commonly called a "Tico" or "Tica") is friendly, hard-working, welcoming to foreigners, and happy (the Happy Planet Index survey classified Costa Rica as the "**happiest country in the world**" recently).

Most Costa Rican families earn less than $10,000 a year. Even a well-educated person might only earn $1000 to $2000 a month. Construction workers, policemen and other similar jobs get less than $500 a month. Yet, almost everyone seems to be well fed, well clothed, and clean, and not lacking in the basic necessities.

Certainly, it would be possible for a couple to live on less than $1000 a month in Costa Rica, with a higher standard of living than in North America, but most foreigners will not be able to do that, and here's why:

1. **You could buy a house really cheap, or rent a "Tico" apartment, but it will be lacking in some basic things that most Western-ers (including me) take for granted. For example:**

    – You won't get hot water running out of every faucet. Running water is cold. For your shower, you'll have a shower heater that gently warms the water on demand, which saves you a lot in electricity but won't be anything like the good hot showers you're used to.

- Most Tico families live packed in small quarters, by American standards at least. A Tico house or apartment may be too small for your needs.

- Tico-quality construction. It's not that the houses are poorly constructed, but rather that the attention to quality and detail is not the same. For examples, many Ticos don't think twice about putting on a tin roof that looks terrible and is quite noisy when it rains (more on noise later).

2.   Ticos have a higher tolerance for noise, but do you?

I found that the average Tico can stand much more noise than the average North American. In many Tico neighborhoods, there's a big problem with dogs barking at any hour of the day or night. The average Tico doesn't seem to care, but personally, it drives me completely crazy! You might also hear motorcycles early in the morning (most Costa Ricans wake up between 5:00 and 5:30 a.m. and are not tiptoeing around just because you like to sleep until 8:00). You might hear fireworks at night, roosters that seem to have lost their inner clock and announce the "day" at around 3 in the morning, and more.

I know some Americans that can live in the middle of all this, and I even did it myself for the experience of living in a Costa Rican community, but habits acquired during years of upbringing in a quiet suburban Canadian neighborhood are impossible for me to eradicate.

I can stand some noise, but dogs barking all night drives me crazy. So like most expats, I live in a quieter part of the country, and of course, I pay a premium for that peace.

3.   The average Tico lives mostly on rice and beans, some meat, and not a whole lot of fruits and vegetables.

You could live on almost nothing in Costa Rica if you ate like a Costa Rican. Then, your monthly food bill would probably not be higher than $150 for two. This would buy you a lot of rice and beans, some vegetables, some meat, and cheap pop. This is not the worst way to eat, but certainly not the healthiest. (They consume a lot of sodium on a daily basis in seasonings.)

Because of my extreme diet of mostly raw foods, with massive quantities of fruits, my food bill is much higher than if I lived on the Costa Rican diet. However, I calculated that I still save about 30-40% on my food costs by living there.

Fruits and vegetables are dramatically cheaper than in North America, and much fresher, too.

However, buying any imported foods will jack up your bill.

4.   The average Costa Rican lives without a car. Can you?

Owning and driving a car is obviously a big expense. The average Tico doesn't own one, because they are too expensive. Brand-new cars in this country are more expensive than in America by about 30-50%, if not more, because of high import taxes. Most people get around by bicycle, buses, and sharing rides.

I did live in Costa Rica for two years without a car. I would occasionally rent one in order to do some weekend trips. But I also lived in a more densely populated area where owning a car wasn't as important.

However, not owning a car can seriously limit what you can do and where you can live. Most nice places are a little out of the way on small dirt roads.

On my last long trip, I bought an old Toyota 4Runner and honestly, it was a great investment. First of all, the beautiful place where I lived would not have been reasonably accessible without a car. The car allowed us to easily shop at the farmers' market, go to the beach hassle-free, visit the countryside, pick up our mail, etc., with enough room for ourselves and all our stuff.

When I left Costa Rica, I sold my car (I will give you some contacts to help you do that at the end of the book) and lost a few thousand dollars in the process.

If you don't want to buy a car for an extended stay in Costa Rica, you could always rent one by the month, or live in an area where you can use public transportation. I will review the best areas to live in Costa Rica in an upcoming chapter.

The good news is that although brand-new cars are expensive, there's a good market for used cars, and they are often well maintained and will last you a long time. With no cold or snow, cars last longer than up North.

So let's be honest:

Most Westerners are used to a high standard of living. There's nothing wrong with that, and obviously you can't expect to instantly lower your standards when you move to another country.

I do enjoy the slower pace of life in Costa Rica, and my life is a lot simpler when I'm there. I don't care as much about the latest gizmo, and I spend a lot more time in nature enjoying simple things.

However, I do also enjoy beauty, convenience, peace, quiet, security, and comfort.

I rented a condo that would be completely out of range for most Costa Ricans, but is quite inexpensive compared to what the same thing would cost in North America (we basically felt like we were living in a little resort, with a pool, and jungle nearby, and a completely modern furnished condo with two bedrooms and modern amenities, for less than $40 a day!).

I drive a car, but spend a lot less time driving than I do in Canada, and more time walking and exercising.

I buy quality food, but it costs me much less than in Canada.

I order stuff on Amazon (like books and kitchen gadgets), and get it shipped to a private mail service with an address in Miami that redirects to Costa Rica and handles customs for a reasonable fee (more information on this a little later on).

I enjoy a great standard of living, but overall, spend about 25-30% less than I would in Canada, and considerably less than I would in Miami, or any other more expensive city in America or Europe (compared to which the savings would probably be in the 40% range).

I could spend a lot less than that if I lived like the average Costa Rican, of course, but then I would be giving up a lot of quality of life.

Overall, Costa Rica is an affordable destination for living and traveling. Basic, but clean rooms can be rented for less than $25 a night, and the mid-range options will give you more for your money than you would get in Western countries. For those considering retirement, a couple could live pretty well on $1800 a month. It would be a frugal lifestyle, but quite luxurious by Costa Rican standards. $2500-$3000 a month for a couple is more realistic for the standard of living most foreigners are accustomed to.

If you own your own house, or grow your own food, you can cut this monthly budget still further by a considerable amount!

Where's the Best Tropical Paradise?

Since my choice was Costa Rica, that's the place I have the most extensive knowledge of. But I did my homework on many others too, and what's best for me may not be best for you. Here are some possibilities to consider.

Whether you're spending one to six months a year in paradise, or making a more permanent move, you need to start evaluating your options.

There are a LOT of places in the world to go, and not all of them will be right for you. The GOOD spots can be generally categorized as follows:

- Places to travel to
- Places to live

For example: the place I've been in the world that resembled my idea of a tropical paradise most closely is French Polynesia, particularly the island of Moorea.

If your idea of Paradise is warm weather, pristine turquoise water and lagoons, white sand beaches, dark blue ocean, amazing coral reefs and diving, tropical fruits and beautiful people, you would love French Polynesia.

I found it an awesome place to visit, but I just couldn't imagine living there long-term, for the following reasons:

- The cost of living (it's more expensive than Hawaii by quite a bit)
- The accessibility (too isolated!)
- Residency/visa options (unless you're French, they won't let you

stay for very long)

So, it is an amazing tropical paradise… but not a very convenient one, and not a good candidate for a permanent move.

Let me review a few tropical paradises, and what I like best about them.

Brazil

Most people don't really consider Brazil as an option for relocating abroad. You don't hear a lot about Brazil, at least not nearly as much as you hear about Costa Rica, or even Thailand.

But I found the country to be amazing for someone considering at least a part-time home.

The flight there is a bit long (about 10 hours from New York), but not as bad as you might imagine. Just pick up a good book, and in no time you'll reach the famous cities of Rio de Janeiro or Sao Paulo.

Here's what I love about Brazil:

Beautiful white-sand beaches. Literally thousands upon thousands of kilometers of the most amazing beautiful beaches in the world.

Fruit, and food in general. The fruits and vegetables in Brazil are some of the best I have tasted anywhere — even better than Costa Rica. The mangoes are amazing, and the pineapples are just divine. Plus: some of my favorite tropical fruits grow there and are commonly sold, such as jackfruit!

Cost of living: Brazil has gotten more expensive over the years, but cost of living can be 20% lower than in the USA.

For example, on my last visit a few years ago, I was in the mountainous area surrounding Rio de Janeiro. Out of curiosity, I asked around for prices on houses. I found a house for $50,000, which included an entire fruit orchard. I'm sure prices are much higher nowadays, but there are many affordable areas.

One of the most upcoming areas at the moment is the city of Fortaleza, in the Northern part of Brazil. It was recently featured by *International Living* as having some of the most beautiful, most affordable beach-front property on the planet right now.

The culture. Another thing I love about Brazil is the culture—the music (think Bossa Nova, and more), dance, literature, capoeira, and the list goes on. Brazilian people are passionate, expressive, smart and friendly. There's even a raw food movement in Brazil.

It's vast! Brazil is almost as big as the United States, featuring some of the most modern cities in the world, as well as the biggest rainforest on the planet. If you like tropical weather, you can locate to the northern part of the country. And if you like European-style surroundings with spring-like weather year-round, the southern area of the country will suit you well!

Beautiful People — Brazilians take better care of their bodies than most people from other nations. Mostly for *vaidade* (vanity), but nonetheless, appearances are important. People work out hard so they can show off their bodies at the beach!

But it also means they tend to be more interested in things like natural living. So Brazil has some of the most beautiful people in the world of all ages (men and women), so if you're looking for love and romance... need I say more?

The country is modern and all infrastructures are in place, including high-speed Internet access.

Brazil has a bad reputation for safety, but this is skewed by the high crime rates in major cities such as São Paulo and Rio de Janeiro. Outside the bad areas of these cities, I found Brazil to be a very safe country.

Overall, the safety level is probably similar to the USA (lower in big cities, higher outside them).

Who It's Not For:

Everyone in Brazil speaks Portuguese, and very few people have a good command of English. So if you're not willing to take on the challenge of learning a new language, then you should look somewhere else as a long-term plan.

Southeast Asia

If you're looking for friendly people, exotic surroundings, beautiful beaches and the best fruits you've eaten in your life, on a rock-bottom budget, then you need to consider Southeast Asia.

But... you have to be willing to make the long, 20+ hour trip from North America (and not much shorter from Europe, although it's within easy reach of Australia).

The best country to consider in this area of the world is **Thailand**, which boasts:

- A variety of residency possibilities
- Modern infrastructure (including great Internet access) and a wide choice of condo rentals
- Really affordable prices

I would love to include Bali here too, as it's the place in the world I have loved the most. But I would classify Bali more as a short-term tropical paradise choice (1-2 months), and Thailand as a more long-term choice.

Here's what I like about Southeast Asia:

First of all, it is dirt cheap! You can live like a king on a poor man's salary here. The only major expense is the plane ticket, but once you're there, expect to pay as much as 4-5 times less for almost everything.

The quality of fruits in Southeast Asia will blow your mind. It's certainly the best place in the world for that. There are also plenty of greens available, and a *huge* variety of delicious tropical fruits. It's also not hard to find unsprayed produce, especially from stands in front of people's homes.

The culture is absolutely fascinating, and the people some of the friendliest in the world.

The beaches are awesome, and the Nature is great, but there's so much more to the experience. Southeast Asia is about the culture, the fruit, and the scuba diving, if you're into that!

Who It's Not For:

You need a certain love of adventure to want to discover Southeast Asia.

If you want to be close to everything, I would not recommend Southeast Asia for the simple reason that you have to travel a LONG time to get there!

It's a very traveler-friendly place, and very budget-friendly, but if you plan to live there eventually, you'll have to do your homework and organize your life so you can be very far away from your family! (Unless you live in Australia, of course!)

Hawaii

Staying within the United States, Hawaii is a popular destination for health enthusiasts and travelers from all around the world. In terms of affordability, we all know that Hawaii is not cheap, but it's not nearly as expensive as some imagine. Generally, food is very expensive, although you can get deals if you buy at farmers' markets.

The Good:

Hawaii is part of the USA, which can be a good or a bad thing depending on your own perspective and goals with relocating to a tropical paradise.

Hawaii is easily accessible, although from the East coast, it's still a 10 hour trip (more from Europe!)

Depending on the island, there can be a lot of great fruit. Organic is also available. There are many small organic farms that take worktraders or WWOOF-ers, who work a certain number of hours per week for room (or screen cabin) and board, often including fresh organic fruit. This can be a great way to check out the place and see if it's for you.

The infrastructure is excellent, and the islands are safe.

There are some great beaches and nature, of course, and varied activities for the traveler.

People speak English.

The Bad:

The high cost of living. Everyone knows about that. Prepare to pay more for everything, except locally-grown foods.

Everything grows really well, which means unwanted things grow well too! Many people have relocated to Hawaii and then reversed their decision because they got so tired of dealing with all the mold and mildew. Weeds grow mind-bogglingly quickly, and some "weeds" quickly grow into huge trees. Bacterial "staph" infections are very common, and can be hard to treat and become systemic. Most worrying for those growing their own produce, a very high percentage of the slugs and snails are carriers of eosinophilic meningitis, also known as "rat lung worm," which is a nematode that can cause an autoimmune response that can wreak havoc on the nervous system, and can cross the blood-brain barrier. This disease exists in Asia too, but the percentage of slugs that carry the disease there is far lower.

In terms of culture, it's not very exotic, and what's left of the Hawaiian culture has been cheapened and commercialized to the highest degree.

It's part of the USA, which like I said, can be a good or a bad thing depending on your perspective.

Costa Rica

This is the country that I have personally selected as my best choice for a second home, and also the country I considered for permanent relocation. Let's review the positives:

Costa Rica is still very affordable. Although it's not dirt cheap like Bali and other places in Southeast Asia, overall the cost of living is 30 -40% lower than in the US.

It's accessible. Costa Rica is actually not that far from the US: only a few hours from Miami, and there are direct flights from many cities in the US and Canada. For many Americans, going to Costa Rica is actually easier than flying to Hawaii.

Availability of organic produce. Although there are huge commercial fruit plantations in Costa Rica, there's also a whole lot of organic, and once you know your way around, you can find some *great* food.

Also, healthcare in Costa Rica is fairly decent, modern and affordable.

Costa Rica is also reasonably safe. There is some crime in the biggest city, San Jose. In the countryside, it feels very safe everywhere. There's no army in Costa Rica, and no war either!

Although Spanish is the national language, English is also widely spoken. There's also a great culture to discover, and the Costa Rican people are very friendly and also generally super-welcoming to foreigners.

But the great plus for Costa Rica is Nature. Don't go there if you don't like Nature. There are some amazing stats about Costa Rica, like the fact that although it only occupies 3% of the world's surface, almost 30% of the country is National Park! The government has done a very good job of protecting nature, and the result is one of the few places pristine enough to call Paradise on Earth. Pristine beaches, amazing waterfalls, the most stunning variety of wild animals, monkeys and butterflies, and more.

In addition to the Costa Ricans being so friendly and welcoming, there is also a big population of expats running very cool eco-friendly, health-oriented businesses and projects.

Since over 1 million people visit Costa Rica every year, and the country's economy is largely fueled by tourism, it's a very traveler-friendly place. You can stay 90 days on a visa issued automatically when you arrive, and renewing it for another 90 days is just a matter of leaving the country for a short trip (for example, to Panama), and coming back.

Overall, the big plus about Costa Rica over other countries is nature.

In that regard, there is so much to do in Costa Rica. You can't count the number of great outdoor activities possible.

At the moment, Costa Rica is still the land of opportunity. You can easily buy land as a foreigner (with the same rights as a local), and even start a business on a tourist visa. The country is still booming, and in my opinion it's one of the best places for any health enthusiast.

Who It's Not For:

Costa Rica is not the USA at half the price. It's still a developing country, and it's also a Latino country. Which means that things take a bit longer to get done than you're used to. You have to be patient, or to learn patience.

It's not as organized and efficient as the USA, which can be a good or a bad thing depending on your perspective. On the good side, it means you're generally left alone by "big brother."

The country's infrastructures have improved a whole lot in the last 5 years, and now it's pretty easy to get around, but it's still not perfect. There are a lot of dirt roads, which makes accessibility difficult in some areas. (But then, that's also true of Hawaii…)

For many expats, that's a GOOD thing, because they don't want a horde of tourists invading their little paradises (and there are still many of them).

Of course, no place is perfect, and Costa Rica is not exempt from that rule. But with the ease of accessibility, the fresh fruits and vegetables, awesome climate, and warm and friendly culture… there's a reason why so many people want to relocate here.

Conclusion

As you can see, you have many choices when it comes to relocating to a tropical paradise.

Sometimes a place sounds really good on paper, but not everything is pretty under the tropical sun! That's why you need a little preparation and good information before you make your decision.

Outdoor Activities in Costa Rica

Costa Rica is a great place for certain outdoor activities. I would not rate it as highly as places like New Zealand, where you can both golf and ski, but it has a lot to offer nonetheless. Also, if you're into sports, there are a few things you should know about Costa Rica.

Snorkeling and Diving — I've been on many diving trips in Costa Rica, mainly near the "Isla del Caño" off the coast of Uvita. Diving was quite enjoyable, although not necessarily comparable to top places in the world like Cozumel or the South Pacific. Costa Rica is not a top destination for divers, but if you love the sport, you can do enough to keep you happy. However, one of the best places on the entire planet to dive is Cocos Island, which is an uninhabited island, reachable only with a 2-day boat trip. The island is part of Costa Rica, and is considered a National Park. It was named the "most beautiful island in the world" by Jean-Jacques Cousteau. Several companies organize diving trips to the island.

Snorkeling is not extraordinary in Costa Rica. Some places offer snorkeling possibilities. It's enjoyable, but there's just not enough coral to see a lot of fish.

Waterfalls and Rivers — One of my favorite things to do in Costa Rica is spend a day in one of the numerous rivers. In the Southern Pacific area (around Uvita), there are so many rivers that can be enjoyed. You can spend all day going from one pool to the next and finding hidden waterfalls! On most days, the rivers are literally deserted, except for the popular waterfalls. It's true paradise! But make sure you put on enough sunscreen to protect your skin...

Fishing — Costa Rica is a great location for deep-sea fishing. In all popular coastal areas, you can book a day of fishing. In many cases, great catches are almost guaranteed!

Hot Springs — I love the hot springs in Costa Rica, especially in the Arenal area. One of my favorite places in the world is the Tabacon resort in Arenal. The hot springs are not sulfurous, so the water doesn't smell bad. Other hot springs are scattered throughout the country as well.

Running & Cycling — The problem with running and cycling in Costa Rica is the lack of sidewalks and the dangerous driving habits of Ticos. For that reason, I would never practice cycling as a sport in Costa Rica, as I would literally fear for my life. As for running, you can usually find a place or park to run several miles.

Surfing — Costa Rica is a really great place for surfing. Most surfers hang out around the Dominical area. I'm not a surfer myself, but I've been told it's excellent, depending on the season.

Besides these activities, you can keep yourself busy with golfing, hiking, and much more.

Costa Rica is not an island, and other things you need to know

"San Jose is a pretty noisy city, so we're looking forward to seeing the rest of the island" is an actual quote I overheard a tourist say when they first got to Costa Rica.

Of course, Costa Rica is not an island, nor is it pronounced "Costa Rico." The confusion probably comes from an island that we all know, called "Puerto Rico."

"I'd love to spend my winters in the tropics like you, but isn't Costa Rica dangerous? Aren't there poisonous snakes?" is another question I often get asked.

I spent many winters in Costa Rica because I love warm weather, beautiful tropical beaches and waterfalls, sunshine, inexpensive ripe fruits and vegetables, and the outdoors.

But Costa Rica (or Panama) is not Miami! Here are some considerations that might discourage you from choosing this beautiful country as a place to live, spend the winters, or retire:

1. **There are bugs at the beach**. Ants are everywhere, and if you leave the smallest scrap of food, they will be all over it. There are snakes in the jungle, and some are poisonous. Mind you, there hasn't been a death from snake bite in over 13 years in Costa Rica, and drownings are far more common, but everybody freaks out about snakes. Yes, there are snakes in the jungle. I once discovered that a 3-foot boa lived in our attic, and one hotel owner I know got his parrot eaten by a snake. They're not after you, but they're out there.

2.   **There are no street numbers and often no street names in Costa Rica or Panama, and no to-your-door mail delivery.** Street addresses, even for businesses, are something like "100 meters North of the Santa Lucia Church". It's up to you to figure out where Santa Lucia church is…

3.   **Don't move here if you insist on things getting done… yesterday!** Latinos don't like to offend, and will often say that things will be done much sooner than they actually will, just to save face. If you like everything to be done in an orderly, perfect way, and get mad at every employee or clerk that makes you wait, you will not be happy here.

4.   **Don't move here if you're the "control freak" type.** When a neighbor throws a party and cranks the music, it would be extremely impolite to knock on the door and ask them to please keep it down. Here, people are expected to be able to live their lives. The good thing is that probably nobody will knock on your door to complain about anything! If they do, it'll probably be a fellow gringo rather than a local. If someone doesn't like your dog, keep it on a leash. Your neighbors will be much more likely to poison it with rat poison than to call the police or complain about it. I am not kidding.

5.   **Again, Latinos don't like confrontation.** It's a culture of "harmony" under smiling pretense. Latinos don't like our version of "honesty," where we confront someone with the truth of their incompetence. Nothing will win you an enemy faster than doing this here. If you ask a taxi driver, "Do you know how to get there?", he might respond, "Si, señor, no problem." That may translate that yes, he knows how to get there. Or that may translate to mean "Yes, I might know how to get there, once I ask a few people and fellow taxi drivers." Or that might in fact mean, "No, I have no idea how to get there, and in fact I'm not even a real taxi driver, I'm just pretending to be one!"

6.   **Don't move to Costa Rica or Panama if you're easily frustrated by red tape.** Something as simple as getting a phone line, opening a bank account, or even getting a cellphone, can be extremely complicated in Costa Rica if you're trying to do it on your own.

I suggest working with an expert in relocation such as the ones recommended at the end of this book. The positive side of this is that rules are not always "set in stone" and you can often talk your way out of something (this may sometimes involve giving a bribe to a city official).

7. **Don't come and live here if you can't learn to relax**. About once a week, the power goes out. You never know when it's going to happen, and what caused it. It usually lasts a few minutes, but can last up to an hour. It has never lasted any longer in all the time I've lived here, but I've also never been able to figure out what caused it. The locals just smile, tell you to relax, "it will be back!"

8. **People in Costa Rica and Panama speak Spanish, and not many outside of the tourist industry can speak fluent English**. If you just come here and talk to everyone in English and expect them to understand, you will be frustrated.

9. **There are no hurricanes here, but earthquakes and volcanos are the local natural health hazards.** You won't be more at risk living here than living in San Francisco, but you have to be aware than the next "big one" could be tomorrow.

10. **Hot water is a luxury.** In most budget places, the water in the shower is "warmed" by a little electric device. These showers are known as "suicide showers" among gringos, although I've never actually heard of anyone electrocuting themselves with them. By the way, I have lived here with hot running water, but I also didn't have it the first three years I lived here.

I also want to debunk some misconceptions about living in Costa Rica or Panama:

You don't need any vaccinations to come here. There are no malaria outbreaks and the risk of tropical diseases is very minimal.

There is crime, but no more than in most major cities of North America (although Costa Rica is battling a growing crime problem, due to drug trade from Columbia).

The tap water is actually drinkable. Both countries are very clean. People are better groomed than the average American, and the average restaurant is very well maintained, cleaner than the average restaurant in the States.

You can get high-speed Internet access in most major cities, and even by the beach. There's an Internet café on almost every street block (often costing less than $1 per hour).

Your cellphone will work here.

There is no army, no civil war, no guerilla groups, and a very peaceful political climate.

Don't let the minor annoyances put you off! Living in Costa Rica has so much to offer. The dream of the tropical paradise is a reality! Warm weather, friendly people, beautiful waterfalls, low cost of living… just don't try to go it alone.

Costa Rica Has No Reason to Envy Its Neighbor!

A lot of people are looking for the "Next Costa Rica." They're longing for the days when $10,000 would buy you several acres of beautiful tropical paradise in Costa Rica.

Now everyone says that "Costa Rica is overpriced" (which is not true), and many people start looking elsewhere for the next Costa Rica.

Nicaragua is starting to attract some attention, because land is much cheaper there than in Costa Rica, and the country is still several years behind Costa Rica in development.

But let's ask ourselves… why is Costa Rica popular?

Is it just because the country put out a lot of PR and everybody decided to buy property there?

Or is it because Costa Rica has something its neighbors never had, and probably never will have in the future, which is: political stability, personal freedom, peace and democracy?

Let's take a look at the situation in Nicaragua.

A socialist, increasingly totalitarian government called the Sandinistas, led by Daniel Ortega, is currently ruling Nicaragua.

Like Chavez in Venezuela, Daniel Ortega is working on changing the constitution to allow him to remain in power for longer.

The best proof that life is not so great in Nicaragua and that things are NOT about to get better, is the fact that thousands of Nicaraguans are seeking refuge and better opportunities in Costa Rica every day.

Nicaraguans (called Nicas) flee to Costa Rica much like Mexicans or Cubans seek a better life in the USA.

From the blog The Real Costa Rica:

"There are a huge number of Nicaraguans living here in Costa Rica. In fact, there are about eight times more Nicaraguans than North Americans.

"Some Nicas are here legally, but a fairly large number are here without papers. They arrive via passport, then like some North Americans... they never leave."

What's the difference between the two countries?

Costa Rica is simply more prosperous. It has more opportunities, more work, more peace, and real democracy.

Some might say that Costa Rica is also a socialist country, but that's exaggerating the reality. It's true that Costa Rica has opted for a big government. But the country also has more economic freedom than almost any other country in Latin America, except Chile. For that reason, it's one of the most prosperous Latin nations.

Yes, there are a lot of state-run monopolies, and all of them are pretty inefficient. But there's also freedom for entrepreneurs, which you don't get in a truly socialist country.

The state-run healthcare service is called the CAJA. Costa Ricans can join through their employers, and foreign residents can also join for about $100 per month.

But even though there is a certain form of universal healthcare, private healthcare is permitted and thriving. Doctors working for the public system will often work for private clinics as well.

By comparison, in Canada, doctors can only work for the government, and it is illegal to sell private health insurance.

In addition to this mixture of public and private services and the choice that provides, another important feature of Costa Rica is the lack of an army, and strong national pride in peace.

Presidents can only serve ONE term, therefore avoiding any possible dictatorship. And unlike in Nicaragua or Venezuela, you don't have presidents that get elected and then try to consolidate power in a Hitler-like fashion.

Costa Rica takes pride in its democracy, and even its elected left-wing government is pretty moderate, and works toward developments aimed at improving the country.

I'm not saying that all is perfect in Costa Rica. I'm just saying that the political situation makes it completely different than its neighbors.

I believe it's important to understand a county's politics in order to make a decision to live there. There are so many beautiful countries in the world, with amazing people — that are being completely destroyed by their politics.

Nicaragua is certainly an example. Venezuela is another one. But unfortunately, there are many more.

If you'd like to read a great book on the history of socialism around the world and how it's been an amazing failure that has cost the lives of hundreds of millions of people, I suggest reading "Heaven on Earth: the Rise and Fall of Socialism," available on Amazon.

I recently spoke with an American living in Costa Rica, who moved there from Nicaragua. He told me exactly how he was harassed by the Nica government for not sharing their political views, and how they threatened to take away everything he had for "counter-revolutionary beliefs," or something like that.

It is becoming clearer that Nicaragua is NOT the place to be at the moment, but Costa Rica still is.

Panama vs. Costa Rica

I've been visiting Costa Rica since 2002, and since that time I've spent more than 24 months of my life there. I view Costa Rica as one of the most wonderful places in the world to live in and travel to.

But Costa Rica is not perfect — and no country is, really. Because I was sometimes frustrated by the shortcomings of Costa Rica, I also looked into Panama, Costa Rica's most affluent neighbor.

After three trips to Panama and a lot of research, I think the two countries have a lot in common, but also important differences.

Which place is better to live? It will be up to you to decide, but here are the most important differences:

Pros for Costa Rica

Let's start with where Costa Rica excels.

"No Artificial Ingredients"

Costa Rica has positioned itself to the world tourism market as an "eco-tourism" destination. "No Artificial Ingredients" is the advertising slogan. While it's not always true, I can say that overall there's a lot more environmental awareness in Costa Rica than in most places in the world. In large part, this is due to the influx of eco-loving expats that have bought huge tracts of land in order to protect it.

A lot of the locals have also realized they can make more money by bringing tourists to their area rather than clear-cutting forests or hunting endangered animals. Costa Rica protects over 25% of its territory in National Parks.

Costa Rica is overall cleaner, especially when compared to Panama City. Panama City is three times the size of San Jose, so that brings advantages when it comes to conveniences, but disadvantages when it comes to cleanliness.

San Jose is a pleasant city that looks more like a large, sprawling town. The air is fresh and clean (which wasn't so much the case years ago when toxic diesel fumes filled the air), and also considerably cooler than steamy Panama City.

Beyond "tree-hugging," Costa Rica feels more pristine, and ridiculously beautiful. Panama has many amazing treasures and beautiful areas, but they are more remote and less accessible than Costa Rica, where tourism is a major industry.

More Tourism

Costa Rica gets over 2 million visitors per year, whereas Panama gets just about 800,000 (and a lot of them are business visitors going to Panama City). That's a huge difference, and it shows when you visit the country.

In Costa Rica, literally every beautiful area has been discovered, and there are hotels of all classes to cater to the tourist market. I find that an advantage in a certain way, because there's always something new to do in Costa Rica. I've been coming here for many years, and I still haven't visited every place I want to visit, nor been on every tour or visited every attraction I want to see.

You can't really get bored in Costa Rica, so it's probably a better place to come for a short vacation than Panama.

This also means that Costa Rica tends to be more expensive, and certain popular areas are overrun with tourists. But even in extremely popular places like Lake Arenal, I don't find that to be a problem.

More Expats

More North American expats live in Costa Rica than in almost any other country in the world. The country offered tempting incentives for retirees to come spend the rest of their lives back 20 or 30 years ago. Now most of these incentives are gone, but the country still remains open for retirees, and many take advantage of the warm climate and lower cost of living.

There's a lot of services available for expats, and more opportunities to mingle with people who speak your language, which again can be viewed as an advantage or a disadvantage.

More Fruit

For raw food enthusiasts like me, it's hard to beat the variety and quality of fruit you can find in Costa Rica. Panama has a lot too, but not nearly as much variety as Costa Rica. There are more farmers' markets throughout Costa Rica, where you can buy really fresh produce.

Organic produce is rare (compared to the States), but available if you know where to look for it. In Panama, every type of fruit I tasted was delicious (melon, pineapple, etc.), but the variety is more limited, unless you grow your own or can buy from local gardens.

No army

Simon Black, of the "Sovereign Man" newsletter writes:

Costa Rica has no military. Technically Panama has no military either, but with so many national police (green uniforms), tourist police (tan uniforms), and Presidential guard (black uniforms)

running around the country with automatic weapons, they might as well be an army, albeit a poorly trained, dysfunctional one.

I doubt that the Panamanian police forces have the capability or iron will to go house-to-house against the locals, but Costa Rica lacks the manpower resources altogether.

Pros for Panama

Lower cost of living

Panama is cheaper than Costa Rica, by about 10-25%. For example, a plate of food at a local cafeteria in Panama will cost you around $2. In Costa Rica, the same would be $3-4. A small to medium watermelon at a farmers' market in Panama is about $2. In Costa Rica, it's $3-4 for the same size of watermelon.

The expat and tourist markets in Costa Rica have driven up the prices, so almost everything is a bit more expensive than in Panama, from Real Estate to water bottles.

Also, Costa Rica has a fairly protectionist economy. They derive a lot of their tax income from import taxes on luxury items like cars, electronics, appliances, etc. It's nearly impossible to find a good refrigerator in Costa Rica from a name brand you can trust, unless you go to the tax-free port of Golfito, where you're allowed to get $500 worth of goods every year, tax-free.

Cars are also much more expensive because of these extreme import taxes. Panama also has import taxes, but not as high as Costa Rica's. That's also why almost every imported item is cheaper in Panama.

US Dollar

One major advantage of living in Panama is the US dollar (especially when you are getting paid in US dollars, like me). Simon Black writes:

Panama is dollarized, but Costa Rica has its own currency (the colon); you might think this is a good thing, but the colon is so small and thinly traded that it essentially follows the dollar, without necessarily getting any of the benefits of being the world's reserve currency.

The bottom line is that the Costa Rican colon (CRC) is essentially the worst of both worlds, and in a currency crisis, the country will likely be hit hard between the eyes.

A side benefit of using the dollar is the "change" situation. In Costa Rica, you end up with lots of heavy coins takings up space for all these crazy amounts of colones you have to pay every day. For example, one dollar is worth about 500 colones at the time of writing, and there's no 500 colones bill. So you end up with a large amount of change that weighs a lot, but is worth almost nothing! In Panama, the one-dollar bill and small US coins solves the problem. I love that!

Way Better Infrastructure

The current president of Costa Rica, Oscar Arias, recently said, "We're a country of five-star hotels and one-star highways."

He's exactly right in admitting a big shortcoming of Costa Rica: the infrastructure. But I can say that in the last 6 years, the roads have improved at least 200%. They still can't compared to the excellent, Americanized roads of Panama, though.

Costa Rica is also burdened by a centralized, socialized public utility company called ICE (pronounced EE-SAY) that handles everything from cellphones to electricity to the Internet. It handles everything… poorly!

The cellphone system in Costa Rica is at least 5 years behind the rest of the world, and even though the Internet works and you can get high-speed connections, truly fast Internet (in my book: 3+ MB per second) is impossible to find in most areas.

If one day your Internet crashes and you need help from ICE, all I can say is "good luck." I've been lucky because I've rented places where the owners would handle the situation and wouldn't mind standing in line for hours at ICE's offices, but others have often waited several weeks to get someone to come over.

Want to get a cellphone in Costa Rica? Good luck, if you're not a resident. You'll need to open a local corporation and put the cellphone in the corporation's name. Same for many utilities, which are difficult to get as a non-resident.

What about in Panama? Just walk to the cellphone store and walk away 30 minutes later with your own functioning phone!

Less Bureaucratic

Panama is overall less bureaucratic and more business friendly. It's still quite corrupt, like most Latin American countries, but getting things done is easier.

It's also easier to immigrate to Panama and get your residency under a variety of programs.

Other Random Differences

Here are other little differences I noticed between the two countries.

Safety: I cannot say for sure which country is safer. But I can say that Costa Rica is currently fighting a rising crime situation. Although I've never had any problems myself and I feel safe even in San Jose, increased crime seems to be a problem. I cannot tell for sure whether Panama has more or less crime, but some people say that Panama is at least better at fighting it.

Taxi: The taxis are definitely better in Costa Rica. They use a meter (and are obliged to do so by law), so you know what you're paying. In Panama, there are no meters, and unless you know the exact fare, you can easily get ripped off.

Noise. In Panama City, there's a big honking problem. All drivers seem to be angry and impatient, and constantly and madly honk. Costa Rica is at least 1000% better. However, Costa Rica has more dogs that bark all night.

Society. Panama is a more conservative society, whereas Costa Rica is more Americanized in that regard. In Costa Rica, women wear provocative and revealing clothing (which does not suggest that they are promiscuous, it's just the local trend), whereas this would be frowned upon in Panama. In Costa Rica, you can wear shorts in the city and nobody will look at you twice, whereas in Panama wearing shorts in the city will quickly label you as an ignorant tourist, or a hobo.

Both countries have a lot to offer. You know how I ended up choosing: this comparison should help you decide which way you will choose.

Choosing Your Climate in Costa Rica

NOTE: You might want a map for the rest of this chapter! Due to copyright reasons, I could not include a decent, detailed map of Costa Rica in this book. I suggest opening your iPad or computer to Google Maps to get an idea of the locations of the cities I will discuss.

One thing that constantly amazes me about Costa Rica is the variety of climates and sub-climates within the same small country.

Back home in Quebec, the only thing I knew in terms of sub-climate was "cold" and "colder." For example, Montreal was cold, but Quebec City was a few degrees colder.

I was also aware of a small island near my hometown with a particularly warm sub-climate where they could grow grapes for wine. However, both the grapes and the wine didn't taste very good…

When I first arrived in Costa Rica in 2002, I wasn't aware of the variety of sub-climates. Like most newcomers, I thought that the capital, San Jose, had a rather mild climate.

And indeed, it does. At nearly 4000 feet in elevation, the city enjoys a year-round spring type of weather. Daytime temperatures are usually in the low 70's (or 22-24 Celsius), with nighttime temperatures just a bit cooler.

Do you enjoy springtime temperatures? Some people really do, and that's why they settle in San Jose, or more likely in nearby Escazú, where a lot of foreigners have chosen to establish their homes.

I read that Escazú is even slightly cooler than San Jose. I didn't find that to be true, although it may just be because the few degrees didn't make a perceptible difference.

If you want to stay in the Central Valley, but like it a bit warmer, more like "summer," then go to the nearby airport town of Alajuela. When it's 72 in San Jose (22 Celsius), it might be 80 in Alajuela (27 Celsius). But even with that summery temperature, nighttime in the mountains is always cooler and comfortable, with no need for air conditioning.

Santa Ana, which is on the road to Escazú and almost part of the same town, is also warmer, being lower in elevation, like Alajuela.

Who's Got the Best Climate?

Many inhabitants of Costa Rican towns like to boast about their specific climates. When I visited the town of Atenas, which is still in the Central Valley, but on the road to the Pacific, I saw many signs posted that claimed the city had "el mejor clima del mundo" — the best climate in the world. The claim is apparently supported by an article that appeared in National Geographic in the 1990's. Nobody has ever been able to quote the article directly or reprint it anywhere, but every single guidebook I've seen that covers Atenas will talk about this curious fact.

I found Atenas to be pleasantly warm during the day, and surprisingly cool at night. If you like sleeping with a real blanket (but not a big one), you might like climates like that of Atenas.

As you can see, all we have to do is change elevation by a few hundred meters to get a different climate.

So, how is it by the beach?

The town of Quepos averages 85 degrees year-round (29 Celsius), sometimes reaching close to 90.

When I was living in Uvita, the temperature by the beach was around 85 degrees during the day, with lower temperatures at night (but warm enough to call for a fan).

However, because we lived a couple hundred meters up in the mountains, we didn't need air conditioning. There was a constant breeze coming from the ocean, cooling things down.

In the northern province of Guanacaste, where a lot of beach resorts are located (with famous beaches such as *Playa del Coco* and *Playa Flamingo*), the dry season is really *dry*, with sun every day for many, many months in a row, and daily temperatures close to 90 (32 Celsius).

Even with that type of warm weather, you'll still be more comfortable than in Panama City, where it's often above 90 almost every day, and very humid.

You could also be somewhere in Costa Rica where it can be downright *cold*, which would be above 6000 or 7000 feet in elevation. But even then, it never freezes anywhere in the country.

What About Rain?

Along with weather, different areas of the country have different takes on the "rainy season."

For most of the country, the rainy season starts in May and lasts until the end of October.

A lot of people imagine that it rains all the time during this season. Not so fast! Usually, the mornings are gloriously sunny. Then it will probably rain in the afternoon almost every day. Sometimes briefly; sometimes, for a few hours.

The rainy season is also a very beautiful time of year because everything is green and lush, yet there are no hordes of tourists ruining everything…

Plus, rainy season can also be mango season (which is in July, although mangoes are available throughout the year).

But the situation with the rain varies in different areas of the country.

Generally, the farther south you go, the more green and lush it becomes.

In Guanacaste, in the north, the dry season is truly dry, with almost no rain for almost 4-5 months in a row.

The Central Valley is a bit dry during that time, but still beautiful.

And then as you go south, you'll find that even in spite of the "dry" season, the vegetation is still lush and green during that time.

What Do I Like?

Personally, I like warm weather, but I like cool nights. I also like lush vegetation. That's why I chose the southern part of Costa Rica.

But at this point, I wouldn't live by the beach. I prefer to be at elevation, with cooler nights, and gloriously sunny warm days.

The town and area of San Isidro Del General has perfect weather, as far as I'm concerned.

Low 80's during the day (around 27-28 Celsius), and maybe 62-65 at night (16-18 Celsius). Some people like it a bit cooler, but I find that perfect!

And because it's in the south, the entire area is still lush and green, even during the dry season.

But remember, anywhere you go... you can still fine-tune your climate by changing elevation!

Folks I know who live on the southern coast of Costa Rica, by the beach, for example in Ojochal or Uvita, can build their house in the mountains to get the weather they like best. And when they want to sweat at the beach, they simply drive down for 5-10 minutes, and they're there!

The Caribbean Coast

I've covered quite a few climates, but purposely omitted to mention one: the Caribbean side.

In this area, the terms "dry" and "rainy" seasons don't apply so much. It seems to rain equally throughout the year, for maybe 20-30 minutes every day.

The temperature is warm, but not excessive. And the driest months of the year are apparently September and October, which are the *rainiest* months everywhere else in Costa Rica!

I've visited the Caribbean coast of Costa Rica a few times. It's an enjoyable trip, but I felt that it was too underdeveloped to even consider for relocation. If you think Dominical is underdeveloped, wait until you try living on the Caribbean side! This area may be appropriate for adventure people who want to set up businesses in the tourism or restaurant industry, but I would not recommend it for most people.

I hope I didn't confuse you in this chapter. My point is: Costa Rica is a wonderful place to live, because the various sub-climates offer you lots of choice: there's probably a place with your ideal climate.

You can live in a temperate climate if you like, yet be within driving distance of lush, tropical weather. But you *can't* ski on the weekends and come back to the beach during the week. Which suits most of us just fine...

Barking dogs and other noise considerations in Costa Rica

If you come to Costa Rica in search of peace and quiet, you should be aware that your conception of what is "quiet" will be very different than that of the local culture.

When I decided to relocate permanently to Costa Rica in 2006, it was the end of the rainy season. We had just moved to the town of Uvita, where lush forests surrounded our house.

Over the 8 months I spent in that area (this includes some time back in 2005), I discovered the various "sounds of the jungle."

First of all, there are the crickets, or whatever the hell those things are. If you come to the southern area of Costa Rica during the dry season, you'll be welcomed by the sound of the insects.

It appears that the hotter it gets, the louder they get. And of course this is true, because they're cold blooded, so they warm up as the temperature goes up. In fact, at some times during the day, the sound of the jungle is incredibly loud — so much so, it's sometimes hard to hold a conversation!

You have to witness it for yourself to believe it.

As soon as night falls, the sound level drops by at least 80%! Sometimes, almost instantly.

When I was fasting in Costa Rica in 2005, I was spending all my time in my cabin near the forest.

One day, when I left for the beach, I noticed something… it was so quiet! I hadn't even realized that I had been surrounded by this sound for so long… until I left, and noticed the difference.

To be honest, it was a relief…

I don't know exactly how it works, but it seems that their "singing" acts as an air-conditioning mechanism. During the rainy season, it's pretty quiet, by comparison.

However, this is a natural sound that we can adapt to. Eventually, you don't even hear it. But for a newcomer, it can be pretty annoying.

Keep in mind: you have to live close to the "jungle" to really hear it loudly.

Frogs

In Uvita, our home was open-air. In fact, there were very few real walls in the entire place.

But November was mating season for certain types of frogs. At night, you could hear them making loud, strange sounds.

My girlfriend at the time had her son and daughter living with us. I remember Mika said one night "Mom… I want to *kill* that frog!"

She just couldn't stand the frogs making those sounds all night long.

It was bothering me too, but often I was so tired at night that I would just fall asleep, and not even notice them.

Eventually, though, I wanted a room with four walls and a roof to isolate myself from the sounds of the "jungle."

"That Bird"

I also remember how my roommate in 2005, for a fitness retreat, couldn't stand a particular bird who would sometimes during the night unexpectedly make a jackhammer kind of sound.

I really laughed when he woke up during the night and just said "That F*#$@#P Bird!"

Barking Dogs

Of course, there are the barking dogs. Everyone has dogs here, and apparently no one has ever watched or paid attention to "The Dog Whisperer." It seems like Cezar would have a lot of work here, because people don't train their dogs to only bark for strangers.

This seems to be more of a problem in neighborhoods of large towns and cities, and not so much out in the country, where you have few neighbors close by.

But get used to hearing dogs barking non stop, sometimes for hours on end, in the middle of the night, and no one stopping them.

Strangely enough, this also seems to be related to the dry season. During the rainy season, the dogs are pretty quiet at night. Why? According to an expat I met here, "Because they're freezing their asses off!"

Fireworks

You've been in Costa Rica for a few days, and you're really starting to enjoy your crime-free neighborhood. Suddenly, quite late in the evening, you start to hear a series of *gun shots!* You panic! What's happening?

Don't worry, it's just the Tico way of celebrating every major and minor holiday, a cousin's wedding, or the death of a loved one.

These are "fireworks," but they might as well be called "sonic blasts," because there are few sparkly lights to accompany the sound.

What better way to celebrate any minor occasion?

A Different Culture

If you want to be happy in Costa Rica, you have to accept the culture as it is, not constantly wish it were different.

Most Costa Ricans grew up in small houses, with plenty of siblings sharing a tight space, and are *used* to all the noise that bothers you.

Also, in Costa Rica, you have a culture that favors harmony over honesty, and encourages personal freedom.

It would be considered extremely rude to knock on a neighbor's door and ask him to "quiet down his act" when he's giving a party (a "*fiesta*").

On the other hand, that also means that nobody is ever going to ask you to do the same. The attitude is: you should be able to live your life as you want. And there is no concept here of "noise pollution."

Compare that with where I currently live in Canada, where a very annoying neighbor (not to use another term) knocks on my door every time I try to play any kind of music at a decent (not loud) level.

This is not to say that Costa Rica is noisy and unpleasant. But if you live in the jungle, you can't expect things to be as quiet as a cabin in the woods of Northern Canada. Things are *alive* here, and you'll be sure to hear them.

In the city, the barking dogs at night used to bother me above all else. Especially *one particular* barking dog.

Now, we don't hear him as much, and when I feel I need a good night's sleep and I don't want to be bothered by anything, I just wear earplugs.

My suggestion: before leaving for Costa Rica, buy *several* pairs of earplugs. Try not to live right next to a disco, and enjoy the Pura Vida life!

Where to Live in Costa Rica

Although Costa Rica is a small country — a little bigger than Switzerland — it is vast in its variety of regions and micro-climates.

Because the country is not set up with a complete infrastructure of superhighways, it can take some time to reach one part of the country from another. For example, the driving time from the capital of San Jose to the far-away city of Golfito is around 8 hours.

So when considering different areas to live, I will also mention the approximate driving times from San Jose.

My Top Choices

I've visited most areas of Costa Rica, and I think at this point I can say that I have a fairly good knowledge of the country.

My choices for the best places to live take into consideration what I believe to be the most important values for my readers:

- A healthy place to live, where it's possible to lead the best raw food lifestyle (if you're not into the whole "raw food" thing, don't worry, my choices will still appeal to you on other levels)
- Weather
- Access to modern conveniences
- High-speed Internet access
- Reasonable cost of living

Two Main Choices

You could narrow down your initial choice of a place to live in Costa Rica with one question:

*Do you want to live **IN** the Central Valley or **OUTSIDE** of the Central Valley?*

And the next question could be:

Do you want to live BY the beach or CLOSE to the beach, or do you prefer a mountain environment?

Central Valley: Pros and Cons

Most expats who relocate to Costa Rica settle in the Central Valley, called the *Meseta Central* in Spanish. About 70% of the population lives in this area.

The Central Valley includes not just the capital, San Jose, but all the neighboring towns and cities in this large central plain.

Advantages of Living in the Central Valley

Let's take a look at the main advantages of living in this area of Costa Rica.

The weather: you get spring-like temperatures year-round, with the possibility of fine-tuning your climate by locating to the area that gives you the best weather for you. San Jose has a yearly average temperature in the 70s (around 20-22 Celsius), and some cities, like Alajuela, have a slightly higher, more "summer-like" temperature closer to day-time averages of 80 degrees (28 Celsius).

If you hate hot, humid summers and despise cold, damp winters, you will love the weather in the Central Valley. However, if you prefer summer-like weather, make sure you locate to a town with that kind of climate, such as Alajuela or Santa Ana, or Ciudad Colón.

The conveniences: You will find everything you need in the main cities of the Central Valley, including large, US-Style supermarkets (with a great variety of imported foods and products), the best appliance and furniture stores in the country, the best malls in Central America, the most choice for shopping, the most activities (Spanish classes, yoga, etc.), movie theaters, and everything you should expect in a more heavily populated area.

The infrastructure:. If you live in the Central Valley, it shouldn't be a problem to get a phone line and get access to high-speed Internet, up to 10 MB per second. The same cannot be said of more remote, isolated areas of Costa Rica.

The food. One reason I could consider moving to the Central Valley at some point would be the farmers' market in Alajuela, which is the best in the whole country. Also, supermarkets in the Central Valley carry more products and more variety. If you're into raw foods, you will love the variety of exotic fruits and vegetables available there. There is also more organic food available, and all kinds of ethnic restaurants.

Transportation: Being in the middle of Costa Rica, you have easy access to all parts of the country, either by bus, car or plane. Local airline companies fly all over the country from San Jose. You will also find it easier to travel from your home country to your home in Costa Rica.

Education: You will find more private and specialized schools in the Central Valley of Costa Rica than anywhere else in Central America. This includes bilingual schools, "Waldorf" type schooling, and more.

Overall, you can expect easier access to services, social life, food, and products in the Central Valley, while still being surrounded by beautiful countryside and friendly people.

The Downsides of Living in the Central Valley

Traffic and Population: Because of all the advantages of living in this area, more expats and locals choose to live in this part of the country than anywhere else. This means a higher population and more traffic on the roads. However, you can still find quiet towns where the pace of living is slower.

No Beach: If your dream is to live by the ocean, and go run on the beach every day, you can pretty much forget that if you live in the Central Valley. This doesn't mean you can't go to the beach, but it's something you'll either do on the weekends (if you can drive a car), or as an occasional trip.

The beach is not that far away, but it's not a trip you would make every day. From some parts of the Central Valley, you could be one or two hours away from beaches. A new highway has been completed (extending from Ciudad Colón to Orotina), which cuts down the driving time from nearby towns to the Pacific area.

From San Jose, the beach town of Dominical is about 3-4 hours away. The Caribbean coast is 3 hours. Other parts of the Pacific area can be as little as two hours away.

From the town of Atenas, some areas of the Pacific coast are less than an hour away.

But before you decide that you absolutely NEED to live by the beach, you should spend a couple of months there to see if this kind of lifestyle is really for you.

Beautiful, but not lush, in the Dry Season: If I'm comparing the Central Valley to the southern area of Costa Rica, I find that I much prefer the scenery in the southern area, at least during the dry season. Of course, this will depend a lot on where you are living in the Central Valley. Some areas are drier than others during the dry season.

Living By the Beach: Pros and Cons

If you dream of living by the ocean, don't give up yet. Some of the most beautiful areas of Costa Rica are right by the ocean.

You can figure out the pros and cons by reversing my descriptions for the Central Valley.

For example, let's take the town of Uvita, where I stayed for 6 months in 2006-2007, and for 2 months in 2005.

The area is incredibly beautiful — in fact, it is by far one of the most beautiful places I have seen in the world. I'm referring to the incredible lush coastline, which still felt wild and unspoiled even in 2009 (which is hard to believe).

There are beautiful waterfalls, friendly people, and actually more services than you would expect.

The downsides? Most of the residents there bought land and built their own homes. For that reasons, the types of rental that you and I might be looking for are not easily available.

There's not that much food available, unless you grow your own. You can drive one hour to the farmers' market in San Isidro, which is what many local residents end up doing once a week.

Now there are three completely remodeled supermarkets, but the prices are a bit higher than in the city. Uvita also has its own farmers' market now, but it's very small, and you can find very little in terms of produce.

If you live right by the beach, you will experience hotter weather. Days in the low 90's are not uncommon, but generally it is still comfortable to sleep at night with a fan on. Many local residents prefer to build their houses at elevation, to take advantage of the cooler ocean breeze and slightly lower temperatures.

Here's What I Loved About Living in Uvita

The following can apply to the entire area of the southern Pacific coast:

I loved living by the ocean, and on many mornings drove 10 minutes to go snorkel at "Punta Uvita," before 8 a.m., which is when the guards show up at the National Park and start charging for admission.

I loved running on the beach in the late afternoon for my workout.

I loved living in a small community where everyone eventually gets to know each other.

I loved swimming in the waterfall almost every afternoon.

I loved the incredible beauty of the area.

I loved watching the sunset from one of the restaurants with incredible ocean views, such as Crystal Ballena

Here's What Bugged Me About Living in Uvita

You cannot get around without a car. A car is an absolute necessity. On my last trip, I was glad to have my 4Runner!

Although it is a nice community, this type of laid-back living attracts a bunch of do-no-good, lowlife types of individual whose best concept for living in paradise consists of getting high every day, drinking before noon and breaking beer bottles in public places.

The bugs can be pretty annoying. The loudness of the critters in the jungle is almost overwhelming at times. At some times of the year, you get an invasion of weird, almost blind creatures that fly everywhere in their last few weeks of living, before they die and a new generation is born. This only lasts a couple of weeks per year.

Internet access is fairly unreliable. For checking e-mails and browsing the web it's fine, but if you are running an Internet-dependent business, you will have to develop a new kind of patience.

It's more expensive overall than living in a city, unless you're the type of bum I described earlier.

So I definitely wouldn't rule out beach living for all my readers, but it's certainly not for everyone. You should live in the area for a while to see if it's for you. After two months, you should get a pretty good idea.

The other alternative would be to live in the mountains, but within driving distance of the beach. For example, in San Isidro, you're only 45 minutes from Dominical, which has an awesome beach as well. It's entirely possible to take a day trip to the beach if you have a car: leave in the morning and come back in the evening.

The bus ride takes more time… it's a one and a half hour trip. But even then, you could go on a one-day trip.

So, now that we've covered the pros and cons of living in the Central Valley and by the beach, let's take a look at my best choices for living in Costa Rica.

Central Valley: Fred's Best Choices

Alajuela

When you first land in Costa Rica, you do not actually arrive in the capital city, San Jose. The airport is located in the town of Alajuela, whose nickname is "The City of Mangoes."

The nice warm air that greets you when you arrive heralds the beautiful Alajuela weather, which is warmer than San Jose by a few degrees. When it's 72 in San Jose (22 Celsius), it will usually be 82 in Alajuela (28 Celsius). However, it rarely gets much warmer than this.

So if you're more partial to summer-like temperatures, you will love the climate in Alajuela.

The city is pleasant, and much less expensive than areas popular with expats, such as Escazú. Rentals can be found starting at around $200 per month, and great deals are always advertised in the local newspapers. You can buy a house for $80,000 and up.

Why is Alajuela called the "City of Mangoes?" If you go to the central park in the middle of the city, you will see lots of mango trees planted there. Once a year, around July, I hear they have a Mango Festival. I hope to check it out some time in the future!

You don't have to live right in the center of the city, but can stay in the surrounding area.

Alajuela also has what I consider to be the BEST farmers' market in Costa Rica, every Saturday. The quality of produce is just amazing (with the BEST mangoes I have tasted in Costa Rica), with lots of exotic produce featured every week.

If you don't live in Alajuela, you might consider making the trip once a week to this farmers' market (as long as you are reasonably close).

Heredia

Still north of San Jose, you will find the beautiful town of Heredia, which is the capital of the province by the same name.

I stayed in Heredia for a week back in 2005, and enjoyed going to the central market every day to buy my fruits and vegetables. There was an incredible variety, at great prices.

Heredia is cooler than Alajuela, featuring similar spring-like temperature to San Jose.

There are nice neighboring towns. I personally enjoyed visiting the "Monte de la Cruz," which is higher in elevation, where the countryside reminds me more of Europe than Central America.

Even if you're not going to live there, I would recommend checking out Heredia and its surrounding areas on your trip.

The prices for this area are similar to Alajuela, which means that a lot of affordable housing is still available.

Escazú & Santa Ana

West of San Jose, you will find the "Miami" of Costa Rica: Escazú, which is the most popular city for expats and wealthy Costa Ricans.

Escazú has spring-like weather, similar to San Jose, perhaps slightly cooler.

There, you will find one of the biggest malls in the country: the Multi Plaza, as well as an endless chain of American franchises. In some areas of the city, you will almost feel like you're back in the United States.

The supermarkets are well stocked with imported and exotic produce and products. And if you are into "alternative" lifestyles, you will find everything from yoga classes to Buddhist study groups.

I think this area would appeal mostly to parents who want the best schooling for their children, or people who are not interested in learning Spanish and prefer to stay in an expat enclave.

Personally, I could not imagine living there full-time, although I enjoy staying at a great B&B I often visit on my trips to Costa Rica when I first arrive, which is Casa Laurin, in Escazú (at **www.costa-rica-bed-and-breakfast.com**).

West of Ezcazú, you will find "the next Escazú," which is the booming town of Santa Ana.

Santa Ana has warmer weather — similar to Alajuela — being lower in elevation. In both areas, prices are similar, and tend to be at the high end.

Bargain deals are rare, but you can find rentals for around $400-500/ month, with luxury condos for $1500 and over. Real estate prices for homes start at over $200,000 in most cases.

Grecia, Sarchi, Zarcero

Still in the province of Alajuela, but a bit farther north-west, you will find a series of pretty, less Americanized towns.

One that is becoming popular with expats is Grecia, which at first looks like many other similar towns of that size, but seems quieter and has a more "True Costa Rica" feel than many other places in the Central Valley.

You'll find everything you need there, including a brand-new mall with a movie theater.

You're not that far from Alajuela, in case you want to go to the farmers' market, but will enjoy quieter settings and access to the entire northern zone, which is a really beautiful part of the country.

Aerocasillas, a service that you can use to receive mail from the USA, now has offices in Grecia. I will describe this service later in the book.

Personally, in my travels to this area of the country, I preferred the more quaint town of Sarchi, which is mostly known for producing some of the country's best furniture and wooden artwork.

Zarcero is also a very pretty place, with the most beautiful park in Costa Rica.

If you'd like to be in the Central Valley but away from big cities, you should consider checking out these towns and this area of the country.

Atenas

On the road to Orotina, which leads straight to the Pacific coast and the beach-town of Jacó, you will find the town of Atenas.

Its claim to fame is its climate, which apparently has been judged to be one of the best in the world, as I mentioned earlier.

The climate is indeed nice, with warm sunny days, and nights cool enough for a blanket.

A number of expats have settled in this town or in the areas around it, and enjoy it tremendously.

For me, the biggest draw about Atenas, besides the climate, is the fact that it's very close to the town of Orotina, which is the best place in all of Costa Rica for fruit. The farmers' market in Orotina is every Friday.

The town of Atenas seems very pleasant, although I have not stayed there overnight. I recommend you check it out on your travels.

SOUTHERN ZONE & Beaches

San Isidro Del General

Most guidebooks will mention the town of San Isidro Del General as a "gateway" to either Dominical, or the Chirripo National Park.

Although San Isidro seems lacking in attractions, it's a great place to live long-term.

Please note that the town is more often referred to as "Perez" by the locals, from the name of the county, "Perez Zeledón."

San Isidro is the largest town in the southern area of Costa Rica, but is still small by North American standards.

You're about 45 minutes away from Dominical (or 35 minutes if you drive fast), but have access to many more conveniences, such as banks, supermarkets, a brand-new mall with a 3-screen movie theater, and more.

Aerocasillas also now has offices in town, and generally you can find almost everything you need without going to San Jose.

Speaking of which, San Isidro is about 3 hours away from San Jose. Buses leave every hour from the Musok station.

When you arrive in San Isidro, the city might feel a bit too congested and noisy for you. But keep in mind that the surrounding areas are quieter.

The city has a very Costa Rican feel, with very Costa Rican prices. In fact, you'll find some of the lowest rentals and prices for real estate. But very few people speak English.

The town also has a great "Polideportivo," which is a sports center, with a large running track, trees, a soccer field, basketball and tennis court, and more.

The weather in San Isidro is similar to Alajuela, which is summer-like year round (with low 80's during the day, and somewhere in the high 60's at night, or 28 Celsius during the day and 18 Celsius at night).

I personally find this kind of weather absolutely perfect. But if you find it a bit too hot, you could settle in the nearby town of Rivas, which is smaller and a bit cooler, being higher in elevation.

San Isidro del General is a good compromise for those wanting to have access to more services, but still be in driving distance of the South Pacific beaches.

It's also worth considering any of the communities and towns on the road from San Isidro to Dominical.

For example, the town of Tinamastes is a bit "hippie;" it even has a raw food restaurant and community led by Eric Rivkin (whom you can contact at: **emrivkin@gmail.com**), and some of the most beautiful waterfalls in the country.

Living in one of these towns, you'll be in nature, yet not too far from a bigger city (San Isidro), and not too far from the beach.

The farmers' market in San Isidro is every Thursday, and wraps up on Friday morning (with much less available on Friday). Although not as impressive and well stocked as the Alajuela market, it still boasts a very decent choice of fruits and vegetables, mostly coming from local communities.

Uvita

I'll skip the town of Dominical, which I find a bit too "hippie" for my tastes. Plus, real estate prices are higher there than in Uvita.

About 15 minutes south of Dominical, you'll find the small town of Punta Uvita, next to the National Park of Ballena.

I already told you a bit about this area. But here's some more:

In the last 2-3 years, Uvita saw an exceptional mini "boom," which tapered off with the economic crisis. This brought a new Corona supermarket, and many new stores and houses. Although some locals are afraid the area will become "overdeveloped," it's highly unlikely it will become a big thing like Jacó up north. If anything, the new developments make it easier for people to live there year-round.

The National Park "Marino Ballena" makes it impossible for big developers to create too many resorts and condos by the ocean. The beaches are very beautiful, and there's even a nice spot for snorkeling at what we call the "whale's tail" (because the rocks are in the shape of a whale's tail).

I recently heard from the original owner of the popular hotel "El Tucan" that property prices have dropped in this area, due to the economic crisis.

A year ago, it was impossible to get an ocean-view lot for less than $150,000.

Now, you can get one starting at $50,000.

73

There are a few rentals in this area, but generally they're not suitable for someone running an Internet-based business. The vast majority of expats living there have bought their own houses.

If you go to Uvita, watch out for unscrupulous real estate scammers. Many properties are for sale as shady deals, above their true market values. One such scammer, German-born Patrick Schindler, has stolen hundreds of thousands of dollars in many such deals, and continues his activities with impunity. The local hotel "Cascada Verde" is owned by this bandit, so I would recommend staying away from it.

Ojochal

About 15 minutes south of Uvita is a unique little town called Ojochal. In some ways, it's much nicer and more affluent than Uvita.

A great majority of the expat population here is French Canadian. That certainly got me interested, because I'm a French Canadian myself.

Apparently, many years ago some wealthy French Canadians bought a lot of property in this area, and advertised exclusively in Quebec to sell the lots. Since almost everybody who bought them liked and kept them, they didn't need to advertise anywhere else.

You'll even see some signs in French in the town itself, and many businesses are owned by French Canadians, but also other nationalities.

The area is known as the "Gourmet Town" of Southern Costa Rica, due to a number of exceptionally good French restaurants, such as Exo-Tica. It's close to one of my favorite beaches in Costa Rica: Playa Ventana.

Prices in Ojochal are similar to Uvita, if not higher. But many deals can be found in this area, as some expats try to sell their homes in a depressed real estate market.

Coronado

Even farther south, there's another very small town called Coronado.

Keep in mind that the entire road from Dominical to Coronado and beyond was only paved in 2003 or so! It used to take one and a half hours to reach Coronado from Uvita. Now, it takes about 30 minutes.

Coronado and the surrounding hills are reminiscent of Uvita, but underdeveloped in comparison. There are beautiful waterfalls and amazing ocean views.

It's not next to any beach, but is within 10 minutes of Playa Ventana, and close to Uvita and Ojochal.

Real estate prices are more affordable here, being off the beaten path. Also, it's very close to the cities of Cortez and Palmar Norte, the next biggest cities in the area after San Isidro (which is one and a half hours away).

There's a private hospital and clinic in Cortez, as well as many banks and services.

Plus, when the international airport in Palmar Sur is completed, you will be able to fly there directly from the USA, and then drive 10-20 minutes and be in Coronado! Most likely, though, very few flights will be offered.

If you'd like to explore this area, I recommend staying at the Mango Tree Spa. More info at: **http://www.themangotreespa.com/**

Other places to investigate

There are other places worth investigating in Costa Rica, such as the Caribbean coast, the Nicoya Peninsula, the southern town of San Vito, and more.

But the choices I've given you are the ones I believe will appeal to most of my readers. And they're certainly a good introduction to exploring Costa Rica!

That's why, if you're going to spend several months in Costa Rica, I recommend that you stay in different places during that time. For example, you could spend two months in the Central Valley, one month in Uvita, one month somewhere else, etc.

That's the best way to be sure of which area of the country is right for you.

Quepos

Another Prime Place to Live in Costa Rica

I must admit that I often used to dismiss the Quepos/Manuel Antonio area as overly touristy and not as beautiful as the southern area of Dominical/Uvita/Ojochal.

But I ended up relocating there for six months with my ex-wife on our last trip.

After investigation, I found the following advantages for living in Quepos:

30 minutes from Dominical — Being in Quepos, I'm now even closer to Dominical than when I was in San Isidro. Of course, local beaches are pretty nice, but if I wanted to go to some of my favorite spots in the southern area, Dominical was just a 25-30-minute drive away.

Another 40 minutes to San Isidro — From Dominical, San Isidro is only another 40 minutes away.

Great Saturday Farmers' Market — Quepos has a farmers' market once a week on the boardwalk near the beach. It's smaller than San Isidro's, but pretty awesome nonetheless. You have to go before noon, because it closes at 1 p.m. We were able to get pretty much everything there, so we wouldn't even need to go to San Isidro for food unless we wanted to.

World-class National Park — The small, deserted beaches south of Uvita are quite nice, but there's a reason why the most-visited National Park in Costa Rica is Manuel Antonio: the white-sand, postcard-perfect beaches are simply stunning, and the wildlife is amazing.

Local airport nearby — Quepos has its own airport, where the local Costa Rica airline Nature Air operates (**www.natureair.com**). From Quepos, you can fly to many destinations, including: Lake Arenal, Drake Bay, Bocas del Toro in Panama, Liberia (up north), Limon, and many others. The rates are not cheap, but are affordable. For example, a one-way ticket to Lake Arenal will set you back $129 with tax. That's a one-hour flight (including a stop in San Jose), instead of the 6 hours it would take you to drive there. The airline sometimes runs specials. Make sure you get on their email list to receive them.

Good roads — Quepos and the surrounding area is better developed. That also means better roads and infrastructure.

Beautiful area — The drive from Dominical to Quepos is pretty stunning. Some areas are amazingly beautiful. Before the road was paved, I wouldn't notice them because I had to focus on the terrible road. Now I can soak in the view, and it's a great one.

On the other hand, some disadvantages of living in Quepos for some people may be:

Hot Climate — The climate is truly tropical here. At least 85+ degrees Fahrenheit (29-30 Celsius) during the day, with a few degrees less at night. I find it takes a little time to get adjusted to this, but if you have a pool, it's quite enjoyable. I would still want to have AC in my office at least.

Tourism — Some people prefer to be isolated, away from any form of tourism. Quepos and the surrounding area is one of the most visited parts of Costa Rica. Yet I find that it still has a good balance of tourists and locals. The most visited part is, of course, Manuel Antonio, which is filled with nothing but shops, hotels and restaurants.

All around, the area is a desirable part of Costa Rica to live in. I would recommend checking it out as a place to live, especially if living close to the ocean is important to you.

The Quepos-Dominical Road is Done!

Costa Rica has become somewhat legendary for the bad state of its roads. It's probably one of the only countries in the world that gets so much tourism (almost 2 million visitors per year), but doesn't have the basic infrastructure, in terms of roads, in place.

When I first visited Costa Rica in 2002, the situation was terrible. Just getting to the town of Uvita was quite an endeavor. The entire Southern Pacific Highway was not paved, and was filled with potholes. Just going from Dominical to Uvita took over an hour.

Since 2003, the stretch of highway from Dominical to Palmar Norte has been completed. It's now a beautiful, modern road. Going from Dominical to Uvita now takes about 15 minutes.

In the Central Pacific area, the roads are also fairly good. Going from Quepos to the beach town of Jacó takes about 40 minutes on this modern road.

However, for all these years, there's been one last stretch of road that was never completed. That is the leg from Dominical to Quepos.

Quepos is a strategic location, because it's near the world-famous National Park of Manuel Antonio. For the longest time, the best and only way to get to this part of the country was from the road to Jacó, from the north.

However, if you ever wanted to go to Domincal, Uvita or the entire southern area from Quepos, you had to face that terrible stretch of 45 kilometers of unpaved, pothole-filled gravel road.

This could take well over two hours of avoiding huge potholes that would sometimes be so big they could almost swallow an entire car. During the rainy season, these potholes would be filled with water, making the drive even more hazardous.

So that meant that people *either* went to Quepos and Manuel Antonio, as well as the central Pacific beaches (Jacó and the north), *or* went to the southern area, to Dominical, Uvita and Ojochal.

Nobody except the most committed visitors really wanted to make that drive in either direction.

Over the last several years, the promise of the "road to Dominical" has been hailed many times.

For one thing, it's the holy grail of real estate developers in Dominical and Uvita. Why? Because when the road is finally completed, the Southern Pacific area won't be so isolated, making it more accessible. In the foreseeable future, this will make the real estate prices boom.

Local residents have mixed feelings about the new road. Some would like things to stay the same. That is: underdeveloped and pristine. They fear that when the new road is done, too many tourists will flock from the north, driving new developments that might spoil the natural beauty of the area.

In any case, the new road has happened, little by little. Every year the locals would tell you that the road would be done within 12 months. But of course, it was never done.

Now the road is completed, and the entire drive from Dominical to the Quepos airport takes about 20-25 minutes.

Will the New Road Ruin the South?

As far as I'm concerned, this new road only means positive things for Costa Rica. I'm much more concerned about *under-development* than *over-development* in most areas of Costa Rica.

Dominical and Uvita are very nice, but the isolation that characterizes these areas makes it difficult to live there. Now, the area is more accessible. In fact, it makes this entire area a much more desirable place to live.

When Costa Rica's third international airport is completed in Palmar Norte (the other two airports are *Juan Santamaria* in Alajuela, and *Libera* in the northern province of Guanacaste, we will be able to fly directly from North America to the southern area, and from the airport to Uvita or Dominical in 45-60 minutes.

Of course, real estate prices might go up. But with more demand will come better services and higher quality of life for everybody.

I personally don't see this area being so developed that it might lose its charm. Keep in mind that the Ballena National Park in Uvita protects a lot of the natural beaches. Plus, the area is still farther from San Jose than the beaches of Jacó or Manuel Antonio, unless one flies directly to the new international airport, which still might not be ready for several years.

Right now, real estate prices have stalled, and it's possible to find good deals in the area. It's also a good, strategic time to buy. If you have some money to play with, I believe an investment in the Southern Pacific area of Costa Rica would be a good move at this time.

My Personal Choice

I've lived for extensive periods of time in three areas of Costa Rica: Uvita, San Isidro del General, and Quepos. I've also visited the rest of Costa Rica extensively.

Although I've always lived near the Pacific Ocean, on my next winter in Costa Rica, I don't think I will settle in this area again.

My situation is a little bit special. I work through the Internet, and even when I relocate to a tropical country for a few months of the winter, I still have to work on my business most days. That leaves me the weekends for outdoor activities and the beach.

The problem with living by the beach is the isolation. The rental market is filled with short vacation rentals that may appeal to vacationers, but there's not much for those wanting to establish themselves there for a few months.

The climate at sea level is also too hot for my taste. I think if I didn't have to work, that wouldn't be a problem. I would simply spend part of the day in the waterfall or the ocean! But when working from home, I prefer a more temperate climate, as I don't like to blast the A/C. Therefore, I think I would probably look at Santa Ana as my best choice for relocation. Alternatively, I might investigate Atenas.

That way, I would have plenty of choice for longer-term rentals, and also be reasonably close to the beach (a mere 2 hour drive) for weekend trips. I also would not need to get a car, since I could get by paying for taxis to go everywhere (taxis are inexpensive in Costa Rica). On weekend trips, I could rent a car or hire a driver. My total transportation costs would still be lower than if I rented a car full-time or bought one.

The Crime Situation in Costa Rica

Petty theft is very common in Central America. That doesn't worry me.

What worries me is organized crime by bands of well-known criminals that will target well-off foreigners, or even Costa Ricans, to steal their cars and possessions.

These criminals, armed with loaded weapons, bullet-proof vests, and radios, seem to be very organized. They target specific hotels or even gated communities, or wealthy homes, and get the job done in a few hours without much interference from the police.

The criminal justice system does not seem to be successful at keeping these people locked in prisons, and the problem persists.

Most of these criminals aren't even Costa Rican, but come from Columbia or other rough countries because Costa Rica is wealthier and crime is easy.

Most of the time, there are no casualties, but the situation is worrisome.

I personally do not worry about the media and their portrayal of crime. However, I'm more worried when I hear from too many people I know who got robbed.

So far, this has only happened to a real estate agent I know, who got robbed at gunpoint in his condo home of Escazú outside of San Jose.

Most of this type of crime seems to be concentrated in the Central Valley. I would personally avoid San Jose, and even the wealthier suburbs of Escazú and Santa Ana.

San Isidro del General and the Southern Pacific are still very quiet, and I wouldn't worry about the crime situation there.

Crime seems to be an annoyance we have to deal, with, but I wouldn't exclude Costa Rica from your travel list because of it.

No school shootings have happened here, and the serial killers that have haunted the USA are not likely to roam around this sunny place. There is still much less violent crime than in some parts of the USA.

But there is definitely more crime and theft, including organized crime, in Costa Rica than, say, in Canada. However, I am told that Canada beats Costa Rica by far when it comes to car robberies.

Legal Presence in Costa Rica

If you were thinking about getting residency in Costa Rica, you should know that a new immigration law has passed, and has been in effect since March 2010.

I have found it a bit complicated to find out the truth about this new law, but I believe the following summary to be fairly accurate. Of course, make sure you check with a lawyer before making any decisions.

Why Should You Get Your Residency?

If you intend on living in Costa Rica less than six months a year, then it's not worth getting residency. This is because the country automatically grants North Americans and most Europeans a 90-day visa. This visa can be renewed by leaving the country for 72 hours and coming back. Most people choose to use this opportunity to take a trip to Panama or Nicaragua.

Technically, the law is not clear on how many times you're allowed to do that. So there are a lot of people in Costa Rica (mostly Americans and Canadians) who have been living in the country for many years on nothing more than a tourist visa, that they renew every 90 days by leaving the country.

Here, they are called "Perpetual Tourists." The government doesn't seem to mind them, unless they are undesirable people in the first place. In that case, immigration officers would not hesitate to deport the person.

Will this change in the future? It's hard to tell. This is a grey area in the new law. I think at the very least they will try to enforce the law a little better, and try to crack down on perpetual tourists working in the country illegally.

There are several reasons why you should get your residency in Costa Rica if you intend living here most of the year. Besides the hassle of having to leave the country every 90 days, you also have no legal status in the country. The tourist visa laws could unexpectedly change, and if you've built a life here, I think you'd find that hard to swallow.

Having permanent residency also gives you the same rates as Costa Ricans for entrance to National Parks, and other perks. It also opens the door to eventual citizenship.

You can also legally purchase telephone lines, cellphones, and other services that are currently restricted. You can also qualify for credit at the bank, and open a checking account (not just a savings account).

Since March 2010, these are the main ways to get your residency:

Pensionado Status — This is for people who are retired and receive a pension from the government, or a private company. Social Security qualifies. The new requirement is now $1000, but apparently also covers a spouse.

Rentista Status — This is for people who don't receive a pension or are too young to qualify (like me). In that case, you must prove that you can make at least $2500 per month for the next five years. The way to do that is by depositing $150,000 in a bank in Costa Rica, and withdrawing $2500 every month. They want you to convert $2500 a month into the local currency, the colon, and keep your receipt for that as a proof. I'm told that's an average, and doesn't have to be done every month. The previous requirement was $1000 a month per person (or $60,000 in the bank). The new requirement now also covers dependents (which means a spouse and children).

85

Having a child in Costa Rica is still a very fast track to residency. Even if both parents are foreigners, the child is automatically recognized as Costa Rican, and through that you can claim your permanent residency very quickly.

Marrying a Costa Rican is still a possibility, but the country intends to go after illegal marriages of convenience.

The "Investor" category seems to be the same. You will need to invest at least $50,000 in a "high-priority" industry such as tourism, or $200,000 in other industries. With this category, you cannot include dependents such as a spouse.

With Rentista and Pensionado residencies, you need to spend at least 4 months a year in Costa Rica, until your residency becomes permanent (which takes three years).

For a single person, the new law makes it much more difficult to obtain residency, unless you receive a pension from the government or a company.

I don't think the new law is a bad move on the government's part. It's still realistic based on the current costs of living here. It just makes it more difficult to obtain residency if you're a single person.

But if you're married with children, you might save money under the Rentista program. Actually, keep in mind that your money is not gone, but simply locked in the bank for a determined period of time and earning you interest.

Should You Set up a Costa Rican Corporation?

If you're going to spend a few months a year in Costa Rica, and plan to eventually buy property there, you should consider setting up a corporation as soon as possible.

There are many types of corporation in Costa Rica, but the most popular are:

The Sociedad Anónima (SA), "anonymous society," which is the most common form of corporate structure.

The Sociedad de Responsabilidad Limitada (SRL), which is similar to the American LLC (Limited Liability Company).

In both cases, the corporation features absolute secrecy.

Although the directors of the company are publicly disclosed, the shareholders of the company are completely anonymous, and the law protects this secrecy.

There is absolutely no way to know who really owns these companies, unless you actually look inside the books of the company, which would be found in a safe-box somewhere, or kept by the lawyers who formed the company.

Both types of structure are easy to set up, costing approximately $600 with a good lawyer.

The first structure (SA) requires 4 members: president, treasurer, secretary, controller. You must have these 4 members, even though only one might have real power in the company.

That's why the law firm setting up a SA will often appoint "nominees" to fill these roles, for simple structuring purposes, even though they have no power.

With the SRL, you can have just one individual (the manager), so in a way, it's much simpler to set up.

There are some minor differences between the two. A good lawyer will be able to recommend which one to use.

Here are some uses for having a SA or SRL in Costa Rica:

Acquiring a cellphone. In Costa Rica, there's a stupid law that restricts cellphone ownership. You have to be a resident to get one. Foreigners cannot get cellphones! But with a corporation set up, you can get a cellphone under the name of the corporation, usually within a day.

The SA or SRL are most commonly used to own real estate. It's much better to own real estate under the name of the company, and not under your personal name. This limits your liability, but also makes selling the property much faster and more cost-effective. To sell the property, you simply transfer the shares in the company to the new owner.

Other assets can be owned by the company, such as a car, or a business. This, again, helps you limit any liability. The best way to do any kind of business is through an SA or SRL.

To set up a SA or SRL, I recommend this law firm:

P&D Abogados

Contact: Bernardo van der Laat

bvanderlaat@pdlawyers.net

www.pdlawyers.net

Bernardo is the person I worked with. He speaks fluent English, and can help you with your legal needs in Costa Rica.

Ordering Online and Receiving Mail With Aerocasillas

One thing that bugged me about living in Costa Rica was that I couldn't order books and other products from Amazon and other online stores. But not anymore!

With a private service like Aerocasillas, you can order online and receive your shipment to an address in Miami. From there, your package will be automatically redirected to Costa Rica within 3-5 business days.

They now have offices all over the country, which makes it a lot easier to use the service. New offices have recently opened in San Isidro del General, Grecia and Playas del Coco (Guanacaste).

Here's how it works:

- You get a private address in Miami, one for packages, and a P.O. box for magazines.
- You order online and get the packages sent there, so you don't pay international shipping.
- Packages are redirected to Costa Rica within a few days. You pay for transport by the kilo, and for taxes and duties. Those shipping rates are lower than what you would pay on your own, because shipments for all their customers are combined together.

For books, the taxes are minimal. For other products, like iPods, they can be very expensive, so it's better to bring these items back from the US yourself.

For example, I once placed an order on Amazon.com. I ordered 4 books. The total from Amazon was $65. I got free shipping to my PO box in Miami.

I received the books in Costa Rica 5 business days later. The total cost with transportation and taxes was $25.

So although it will cost you more, it's still very affordable to receive books, magazines and other products from Amazon and other online companies, especially if you're a book addict like me (and books are hard to find in Costa Rica).

For more information on this service, check out **www.aeropost.com**

How Much Are Internet Services in Costa Rica?

If you're wondering how much Internet Service costs in Costa Rica, here's the latest price list from the state-owned monopoly, RACSA.

Type of Service	Download/Upload Speeds	Price per Month
Basic service	256/128 kbps	$6.97
Basic service	512/256 kbps	$8.47
High-speed medium	1.5 Mbps/256 Kbps	$12.97
High-speed Premium	3 Mbps/256 Kbps	$17.48
High-speed Premium	1 Mbps/256 Kbps	$24.98
High-speed premium plus	2 Mbps/512 Kbps	$34.98
High-speed premium plus	4 Mbps/768 Kbps	$49.98
High-speed premium plus	4 Mbps/1 Mbps	$64.97

The speed are expressed as "Kilobyte per second," with maximum download speeds appearing first. So the fastest connection available at the moment is a 4 megabyte per second line.

Notes About Internet Service in Costa Rica:

These prices are about 50% lower than they used to be just 6 months ago. However, the service is still not the same level of quality as you might find in North America.

I would estimate that Costa Rica is about 5 years behind the rest of the developed world when it comes to Internet service. The blame goes to the state-owned monopoly RACSA, a division of ICE (the state-owned electricity company), which is not very efficient, like all state-owned enterprises.

Recently, Costa Rica signed the CAFTA trade agreement with the United States and the rest of Central America. This is good news, as it will allow some foreign companies to break the monopoly and offer better services.

But it's very unlikely that a company will be willing to invest a lot of money to improve Costa Rican infrastructure, so most likely, advances in internet service in Costa Rica will remain behind the rest of the developed world for a long time to come.

Where I live, I believe our owner pays for the top speed connection. In real life, it gives me a 1MB per second download speed, which is fast enough for everything that I do. The upload speed is also very decent.

I'm personally a strong believer in competition, and I hope that Costa Rica will get their act together, as this is a serious block in their progress.

Getting a Bank Account

Getting a bank account in Costa Rica as a foreigner can sometimes be difficult. I was lucky, and was able to open one through a personal recommendation from a friend. There are many reasons why you should have a bank account in Costa Rica if you plan on staying more than a few months:

- **Allows you to withdraw cash without paying outrageous ATM charges.** Remember: in Costa Rica almost ALL transactions are made with cash. Credit cards are also common, but often you'll be charged extra (because the merchant has to pay 7% per transaction). It's easiest to pay for most of your day-to-day purchases with cash. To avoid keeping a large amount of cash at home, deposit it in a bank account and withdraw it as you need it, using a local ATM card.

- **Automatic payment of cellphone and utility bills.** In Costa Rica, you have to pay your bills on time, otherwise service gets cut off really fast. One way to avoid any problem is to set up automatic payments with your bank. This is especially useful if you're not in the country for months at a time.

- **Establishes ties in Costa Rica.** Maybe one day you'd like to live in Costa Rica for a longer period? It'll be easier if you already have some ties in the country, such as bank accounts you can use.

It's important to keep some regular activity in your bank account to avoid it being closed for "inactivity." The easiest way to do that is to order an international debit card from your bank. Then make a few withdrawals from home once in a while to keep the account active when you're not living in Costa Rica.

The easiest way to open a bank account in Costa Rica is to open it at a bank like CityBank, which has an international presence. Usually, a passport and proof of address is all that is needed.

Why We Left Costa Rica

I spent many winters in Costa Rica. I got married in Costa Rica.

I love Costa Rica so much that I've thought several times of moving there permanently and making it my home base. I looked seriously into completing the process of getting my residency there.

But eventually, I decided not to do it full time. This book is a collection of essays about moving to Costa Rica from the perspective of someone who has tried it and lived there. Yet, I feel that I wouldn't be completely honest with you if I didn't tell you why I abandoned the project of making it my permanent home base. I will still remain a "snowbird" and spend a few months every year in the tropics for as long as I can, but I abandoned the project of moving there permanently.

Why this change of attitude?

Was I mugged in Costa Rica and in fear of my life?

Do I feel the country has become too expensive?

Do I think there's some place in the world that's more beautiful and more pristine?

Actually, it's none of the above.

I feel that Costa Rica is pretty safe, even though I've heard a lot about the rising crime situation in the Central Valley. I've personally never experienced any problem.

As for the cost of living, I've always said that if your goal is to recreate the same exact lifestyle you had back home but for cheaper in a sunny third-world country — you'd better stay home, because that's just not going to happen.

And in all my travels, I've actually never been to a place that's as beautiful as Costa Rica in terms of pure, wild nature.

French Polynesia was the most stunning place I ever visited, but it lacks the amazing lushness and biodiversity that Costa Ricans enjoy.

So why did I not relocate to Costa Rica full-time?

To put it simply: I've realized that I love North America too much. If I was older and retiring, I would probably move to Costa Rica. But at my age (35), I have more opportunities living most of the year in Canada than I would in Costa Rica.

Don't get me wrong: there are lots of things I love about Costa Rica, Panama and all these other beautiful developing countries. But I'm just not ready to make one of them my home base yet.

Before I go into my reasons for not making any of these tropical paradises my home base, let me first review what I like about Costa Rica:

- **The climate can't be beat, as long as you live in higher eleva-tions. The weather by the beach is too hot and sticky, with bugs and ants watching your every move. But in the Central Valley or the mountains, the climate is a dream, with year-round spring-like temperatures.**
- **People are very friendly and welcoming to foreigners.**
- **The country is wonderful to visit and there are so many great things to do: visit volcanoes, parasail, canopy tours, scuba dive, hike, etc. If you're on vacation, you cannot be bored; the country offers so much more than just laying on the beach and doing nothing. Each part of the country is different, with over 16 dis-**

tinct micro-climates.

- It's still very affordable compared to North America or Europe, or even many tourist destinations, if you know where to look. Many things are cheaper, including produce, rent, taxis, etc.

- Tropical fruits are incredible, and you can go to many farmers' markets, talk to the growers, and everyone is very friendly, offering you deals, giving you free produce with purchase.

- Animal sightings are almost guaranteed on a daily basis. We had beautiful Titi monkeys visit us regularly (the rare and smart squirrel monkeys); we saw giant iguanas, toucans, sloths, etc.

- The country is very beautiful. Amazingly beautiful, in fact.

I think Costa Rica, Panama and other countries such as Ecuador (where I've never been) have a lot to offer, and I could easily imagine myself continuing to spend several of the winter months in places like that each year.

Even up to three months, you can easily relax into the fact that your stay is temporary, and enjoy what the place has to offer that is different from your home country.

But as you move into longer stays (three months and longer), you start to realize how different the culture is and what the challenges are for living there long term.

I am not your typical tourist. I speak relatively fluent Spanish, I know the ins and outs of Costa Rican culture, I know my way around most of the country, I know the cultural faux-pas, I read many books about Costa Rican history and culture… and I'm very open-minded.

And in spite of this, I've abandoned any project of establishing a long-term residence in Costa Rica, or in its more modern neighbor, Panama.

Here's what's on my mind:

1- Cost of Living — First of all, I think that cost of living can be a very relative thing. A busy Internet Marketer like me does not need a lot of the same things as a retired (expat) English teacher.

I wasn't going to move somewhere just to save money, but what I found is that even though there are lots of things that are cheaper in Costa Rica (such as fruits and vegetables!), imported products are more expensive.

For a few years, I did indeed save a lot of money any time I was in Costa Rica. But that's because I was single and living in a tiny apartment that I rented for almost nothing, and I didn't drive a car, and returned to Canada after four months so I didn't need to buy many things for the long term.

Many things are cheaper in Costa Rica, like fresh produce, rent, housing, and labor-oriented services such as house-cleaning, taxis, etc. But everything else, from electronics to gasoline, is significantly cheaper in the US.

If you lived a simple life in Costa Rica, there's no doubt you would save some money. But if you're young and busy and you want some comfort, I don't think those savings will show. Overall, it will average out to about the same cost of living.

2- Latin Mentality — There's no getting around the fact that people in Latin America are just not as efficient as in North America. You can call it "Island Time" or "A Different Pace of Living," but the fact of the matter is that a lot of things don't really get done very well.

From getting a decent internet connection to regular errands such as banking, the bureaucracy and inefficiency can be frustrating.

A lot of Ticos (Costa Ricans) will be the first to point it out themselves. I remember a taxi driver who kept ranting about Costa Rica being a "culture of mediocrity."

You can criticize a lot of things about Western culture, but I do think we know how to get things done in reasonable time frames, and with the least amount of headaches.

Personally, I wasn't bothered that much by the inefficiency of the Latin culture. I actually got used to taking my time. But in some key areas, it was annoying:

Internet Service. It's hard to get fast Internet service in the first place, and when you manage to get it, it might mysteriously stop functioning at the most random times, and there's nothing you can do about it. Just reset it and cross your fingers it will start working again shortly.

Power Outages. Again, the power can go out once a week or so at a random times, with no explanation. Usually it's for less than an hour, but it's still annoying when the timing is wrong. No power means no lights, no fan, no internet, and in a hot climate, this can be frustrating, and you don't really have anywhere else to go.

Those problems were mainly caused by my choice of location. As I mentioned previously in the book, living by the beach has its disadvantages. On any future trips, I will be staying in the Central Valley.

Food Selection and Shopping.

Because I eat a vegan diet, with a lot of raw foods, quality and selection of health food products and produce is very important.

Again, a lot of people who have never left the US or Canada complain that the food selection sucks in their respective countries.

The reality is that North America (and other Western countries such as the United Kingdom) have the best food selection in the world, period.

In Costa Rica, I must admit the local fruits are delicious. But you are usually limited to the basic varieties of pineapple, banana, papaya, watermelon and mangoes. Everything else is seasonal (including mangoes, but they are available half the year).

When it comes to vegetables, the selection is not that great outside of larger supermarket chains such as Auto-Mercado, which are more like a small high-end market in the US.

You can still get most of what you need, but the selection in North American stores is way better. Also, you might think that organic food is widely popular in Costa Rica, but it's not the case. Most of the beautiful fruits you see are grown with generous amounts of pesticides, and organic food is hard to come by, unless you know some growers or you grow it yourself. The heat and insects pose a number of problems for farmers, and they're not as informed about safe farming practices.

As for health-food stores, they are non-existent in Costa Rica. The closest thing they have to a health food store are these mini-stores called "Macrobiotic" stores (which have nothing to do with the macrobiotic diet) selling all kinds of medicinal herbs and more natural bodycare products, with no food whatsoever.

Some supermarkets carry imported organic products such as almond butter (not raw, of course), but the selection is pretty random, and the products generally cost 20-30% more than in the US.

4- Driving in Costa Rica

Costa Rican drivers have a reputation for being some of the worst and most aggressive drivers in the world, and it's not far from the truth.

The truth is that driving in Costa Rica is an adventure. Streets have no names, and you have to rely on stone-age directions such as "100 meters southwest of the Santa Elena church in the city of Curridabat" — it's up to you to figure out where that is!

I must say I'm impressed to see how Costa Rican taxi drivers know their towns so well, for getting around everywhere without ever relying on a street sign anywhere!

Costa Rica is just not safe for pedestrians. Drivers don't respect anyone's safety and the streets are not designed for walking. There are almost no sidewalks or shoulders on roads, and no pedestrian crossings or lights. Therefore, taking a leisurely walk is just not fun in most places, unless you go to a park.

Driving at night is also not safe because of the poorly lit roads and drunk drivers, and almost every road is a two-way lane.

5- Other Factors

I could go down the list of other minor factors, such as the fact that the sun sets at almost exactly 6 p.m. every night (which is not as fun as a later sunset!), but the main factors for me are the ones that I have discussed, and also isolation.

I love big cities, and I also love nature and the country.

The best situation is when you can take advantage of both.

The dream of relocating full-time to a tropical paradise is a pipe dream for most people.

Hopefully, that's never been what I've promoted. My books and my approach has always been about generating passive income from your online business so you can live anywhere you want, and travel to the place you want, when you want to.

Some people might say, why not Panama? Why not Thailand?

I love all these places... but only to visit a few months at a time.

After my last long visit to Costa Rica, I travelled the world for almost a year. It was a wonderful experience to visit over 25 countries.

After our trip, we decided to relocate to the city of Vancouver (BC), where we've been for about a year.

The climate in Vancouver is pretty mild compared to Quebec, where I'm from. Last winter, we left for the tropics for two months. This was enough to avoid the worst of the rainy BC winter! In Quebec, I needed to leave for at least 3-4 months to avoid the dreadful cold period of the year.

We'll continue to travel many months during the winter to tropical countries… but for now I've abandoned any idea of relocating to any of these places permanently.

How do we manage this lifestyle? If you want to find out about my method for building an online business that gives you complete freedom to travel and do what you love, go to www. dowhatyouloveuniversity.com/new.html and sign up for a trial membership of my Success Group program. You'll get over $1700 worth of products that you can put to immediate use to make your dreams a reality!

The Snowbird vs. the Expat Lifestyle

I meet a lot of people who dream about moving to the tropics. Many imagine that their lives would be a lot better if they left for one of the countries I mentioned in this book.

If you feel the itch to move to warmer climes, you should first investigate whether you're truly meant to become an expat, or you'd rather enjoy the best of both worlds as a "snow bird."

Becoming an Expat

When I talk about becoming an expat, I'm referring to moving full-time to a developing country. Of course, we could apply the term to moving to any country other than your own, but for our discussion, we'll evaluate the specific challenges of moving to those cheaper, more exotic countries.

Moving from Canada to the USA, or vice-versa, is generally not a big change, as those two countries share similar cultures and infrastructures. Even moving to Europe or Australia would not be so dramatic for North Americans.

Generally, what's attractive to most people wanting to relocate to a developing country is the lower cost of living, combined with some other attraction, like the weather.

Most people decide too quickly that they want to move permanently to another country.

The problem comes from the fact that people *fall in love* with the new country and stop thinking with their heads! Instead, they follow their "heart," often making a big mistake in the process.

When you visit a country for the first time, you'll either love it or hate it. But in either case, your perception is that of a tourist. You actually have no clue what it's *really* like to live there.

That's why all relocation experts say you should spend at least 6 months in the new country before you decide to do something drastic, like moving your belongings, or worse, buying a home.

But still, nobody listens! I made the same mistake in 2006, when I decided to buy a place in Costa Rica without doing my research, a decision that I bitterly regretted later.

I *twice* decided to try to move to Costa Rica permanently. But the second time around, I was more careful, and I did not get invested in any real estate deals. Instead, I simply rented a place for six months, while investigating my options for living there.

Typically, new expats will go through three main stages:

- **Falling in love**. During this stage, you love the new country so much that you overlook the shortcomings. Very similar to falling in love with a person!
- **Hating it**. After a few months, you'll probably go through a phase where you start dealing with the cultural differences. This can leave you pretty frustrated and lost, as you try to deal with it.
- **Acceptance**. In the last stage, you come to either accept your new country, or reject it and leave.

Six months is usually enough to go through all these stages. At the end, you'll realize whether you're cut out to be a full-time expat, or perhaps more a snowbird. Maybe you'll also realize that you prefer life in your home country, period.

The expat lifestyle is best for two categories of people:

- **Retirees.** When you're retired, it makes sense to seek a place with a low cost of living and a sunny climate where you can enjoy life.
- **Adventurous entrepreneurs.** If you're young, you could still become a successful expat, as long as you have a job in your new country, or start a business. If you do start a business, it should be the type that enables you to connect with the local community (like a restaurant).

The tricky category of person that may not do so well as an expat is the category I found myself in. That's self-employed people.

I own a small business in Canada, where I sell books and other information products on vegetarianism and health. My products are sold online, and therefore I don't necessarily need to be tied to a specific location.

I thought that moving to Costa Rica made sense, since I could essentially do the same work anywhere.

The main problem I faced was isolation. Although my work is mainly done alone in front of my computer, I also enjoyed a social life outside of my work that I could not recreate as easily in Costa Rica.

When people ask me about my experience living in Costa Rica, I tell them that if they are considering moving somewhere like that, they should take a look at their *current* lifestyle.

Many people I meet live in cities, enjoy eating in great ethnic restaurants, have a social life, and are busy with other activities. They then envision an idyllic lifestyle in the tropics, away from stress and worry, working behind a computer in the jungle, close to the waterfalls and the beach.

The reality is… if you don't currently live in the country, there's a good chance you won't be the type of person that will enjoy living in the country in Costa Rica. If you do decide to give it a try, you should relocate to a city, and not the countryside.

Don't expect to become a different person when moving to a new country! You will be the same person, with the same interests and needs.

Many people who move to a new country feel isolated from their friends and family back home. The good thing about Costa Rica is that it's not too far away from North America. But if you think that your friends are going to come visit you there, think again! Many people claim they will come visit, but never do.

Being an expat is not for everybody, especially in a place like Costa Rica. It's certainly right for some people, but you have to be honest with yourself and ask yourself seriously if you're that person. The best test is to try living in the country for at least six months without committing to anything other than rent.

The Snowbird Lifestyle

The best alternative for most people is to spend some time in the tropics every year. If you're retired, you could spend six months in your home country and six months abroad.

Many retired Canadians and Americans do just this. For Canadians, six months is usually the magic number, because that's the limit of time they can stay legally in the United States each year (many go spend the winter in Florida), but also the amount of time they need to remain in Canada to still qualify for their healthcare benefits.

I have good friends who spend six months in Ottawa and six months in Cartagena, Columbia, and they love it!

I'm personally not at the stage where I can leave for that much time every year, but I find that I need at least 1-2 months away from Canada to "break" the winter.

Because I now live in Vancouver, I find that two months is enough to escape the worst of the cold season, especially in November and December, which are the rainiest months of the year, with the least hours of sunshine.

When I lived in Quebec, I needed at least 3 months, because I found the climate too cold for my taste during January-February-March!

Not everybody can leave for this much time every year, but if your work is flexible or you are self-employed, it's usually fairly easy to do. The only major problem comes when you have school-age children. But even then, it's usually possible to leave for some time.

Appendix 1:
Name Confusion!

A lot of towns in Costa Rica have the same name. So whenever you are getting directions to a place in Costa Rica, try to get as much clarification as possible on where it is.

For example, there are no less than 6 cities or towns with the name San Isidro in Costa Rica! That's probably why locals usually refer to San Isidro Del General as "Perez," as I mentioned earlier. There are two Platanillos, two Palmares, two Matapalos, Two San Geraldos, and so on and so forth.

When my dad visited me in Costa Rica in 2007, he only knew that I lived in Uvita. Not knowing any Spanish, and not having asked me how to get there beforehand, he showed up in San Jose and asked a taxi driver to take him to "Uvita."

Turns out that there's an *island* called Uvita on the Caribbean side, which is several hours away. My dad ended up there, and then had to turn back and go all the way to *my* Uvita, another 8 hour trip!

So don't make the same mistake… investigate in depth before you go somewhere, and realize there may be more than one place with the same name!

Appendix 2: Checklist of Things to Do Before

You Leave for Paradise

Over the years, I've always felt unnecessary stress before leaving for an extended period of time to countries such as Costa Rica, Brazil or Bali.

The stress came from not being sure I had done everything that needed to be done before leaving.

Did I forget anything? Was everything taken care of?

Just the nagging thought that I might have forgotten to do something important before I left was enough to keep me up at night.

So, instead of going through the same anxiety every year, I compiled a checklist of things to do before leaving to what we're going to refer to as a "Tropical Paradise," with the understanding that this can apply to leaving for a period of time to almost any country.

I will provide some explanations for some items that may not be clear or familiar to you, in order to give some details about those things.

Armed with this checklist, you'll be able to sleep better at night in the week leading up to your departure, and especially during the time you're away from "home."

Not all of these items will apply to your situation, and some necessary items for your personal lifestyle might not be included in this list.

But I tried to make it as comprehensive as possible, including information on special cases.

Checklist of Things to Do Before You Leave

Passport

☐ **Verify that your passport is up to date:** I'm assuming here that you have a passport. If you don't, get one now! But also important is to verify that your passport is not going to expire while you're away. Some countries require that your passport be valid at least 6 months after your entry date.

☐ **Verify visa requirements in your destination country:** Each country has different visa requirements. Some will require you to get a visa before you arrive in the country. Check with your travel agent.

Utilities

If you're leaving for more than 2-3 months, I advise you to cancel or downgrade several services you pay for monthly. This will save you an appreciable chunk of money.

☐ **Downgrade or cancel Internet access:** With Internet access, depending on your contract with the provider, you may be able to turn it off before you leave, and reactivate it when you come back for a fee. Alternatively, you could downgrade to the cheapest plan they have, and not pay any penalty.

☐ **Downgrade or cancel cellphone and phone service.** You are probably under a contract with your cellphone provider. But it's still worth downgrading to their cheapest plan when you're away. You won't be needing your phone much when you're gone, except for checking messages.

❏ **Call your cellphone company.** When you talk to them, also ask if the phone works abroad, and what are the rates for using it. Also, if you have a cellphone that receives and sends data (such as a BlackBerry or iPhone), ask about using it abroad. In most cases, it's much better to turn off that option before leaving to avoid expensive charges. For example, my iPhone works perfectly in Costa Rica, but it costs $3 a minute. So I don't use it there, but I can see who's calling.

❏ **Other utilities to cancel or downgrade:** You might want to cancel or downgrade your cable TV service, and anything else you pay for monthly.

❏ **Prepay electricity, cable, Internet, and other utilities.** If you pay your bills online or through automatic debit, then you should be okay when you're away. Schedule a date in your calendar to take care of your bills. Personally, I prefer to prepay everything for several months in advance, so I don't even have to think about it.

Mail

❏ **Arrange for someone to take care of your mail.** Ideally, you don't want to be receiving ANY mail at your personal address. If you don't already use a PO BOX, get one now! For hassle-free travel, if you're in the USA, I also recommend receiving some of your mail at **www. earthclassmail.com**

The advantage of not receiving mail at your home address is that it won't be an obvious sign that you're gone (with mail piling up). But in any case, if you receive some mail, you'll need someone to pick it up for you and keep it for when you come back. If your bills are taken care of in advance, there should be nothing important in the mail. But there could always be some surprises, so find a good person that you can call every two weeks, who can open some of your mail "live" on the telephone with you, to tell you if there's anything important. If you receive all your mail with **www.earthclassmail.com**, there's no need to do this, because you can scan all your mail online.

❏ **Authorize that person to use your PO BOX.** If you have a PO BOX, you might need to do more than hand a key to a friend. If you receive a registered letter, they won't be able to sign and get it for you. So make sure that you give your trusted friend the ability to receive those packages.

Small Business

If you're like me and have a small business, you will need to take some extra steps to make sure "business is being taken care of" while you're away.

Here's how I do it personally:

❏ **I have a trusted friend receive my business papers.** For the past 5 years, my mother has been the one who has done this for me. She gets all my business mail, and then arranges it accordingly:

- *Most of what I receive are statements.* So those are simply filed.
- *For important papers from the government, she scans them and sends them over to me by email.* I can redirect the scanned copies to my accountant.
- *Checks* — any checks that I receive are deposited in my account.
- *Payments* — most of our payments are made either with credit cards or paypal. But sometimes we pay someone by check. So that's why I leave a few signed checks from an account with limited funds, in case we need to pay someone by check while I'm away.

If you live in the US, I highly recommend using the service at **www. earthclassmail.com** to receive your business mail.

If you regularly get checks from certain companies, ask them if they can direct deposit instead.

❐ **The rest of my business is taken care of online as usual.** I keep an Internet fax number at **www.efax.com** in case I need to send or receive faxes. I also bring a scanner with me (I use the travel-size Fujitsu ScanSnap S1100 and I would not recommend any other brand!) With the scanner, I can sign and fax back any important papers that require my signature.

Car

❐ **Call insurance company to downgrade or cancel insurance.** If you own a car, you probably pay something monthly to insure your car. To save some money, you can cancel your insurance while you're away. Cancel everything except theft insurance. Also, advise your insurance company that you'll be away.

❐ **Store your vehicle with DMV or equivalent.** To reduce your payments in license plates, you might be able to "store" your car when you're away. For example, in Quebec one can simply go online to the SAAQ website to "store" the car, which means that it won't be used for a certain period of time. During that time, nobody can use it, but you'll be reimbursed for the months you're not using your license plates. In the USA, contact the DMV for more information.

❐ **Unplug car battery (day before you leave).** Right before you leave, unplug your car battery. That way, when you come back, you simply plug it back in, and it will probably start. If you don't do this, you will definitely need to boost the car.

❐ **Find a place for the car.** Where will you keep your car while you're away? I personally keep it parked in its normal spot, and a friend of mine removes the snow. If I could, I would definitely park it in a garage.

Health & Safety

❐ **Get international health insurance.** You need insurance coverage when you're gone, for emergencies. The best way to find decent insurance coverage is to contact your travel agent.

❐ **Scan copies of passport, credit cards, driver's license, and insurance record.** Photocopies work great, but with a scanned copy you can keep virtual copies, email them to trusted friends and keep them on a "flash" drive. This will be useful if you lose those items.

❐ **Leave your destination address with a relative, along with scanned copies of everything.** Someone should know where you're going and how to reach you (besides email). This trusted friend should also have a copy of the scanned documents.

❐ **Carry a prescription for your glasses (if you wear them).** If your glasses break when you're away, or if you need new contact lenses, you will need your prescription. If you don't have it, ask your eye doctor to fax you a copy, and bring it along with you.

❐ **Medication.** If you take medications, bring doctors' prescriptions with you, and bring what you need on your trip.

❐ **Bring activated charcoal.** I don't bring a lot with me in terms of medicines (because I believe most of them are not necessary), but I do bring activated charcoal. You can find it in most health-food stores. It can be extremely useful in case of food poisoning.

Being in Touch With Family

❐ **Set up a Skype account and teach your friends how to use it.** The best way to stay in touch with family when you're away is to use Skype. Go to **www.skype.com**. I recommend getting a country or worldwide subscription to be able to call back home at cheap rates from your computer (or any computer). With those subscriptions, you also get a number that people can use to call you.

But even better than this is to teach your friends and family to download and use Skype. That way you can stay in touch for free. Do this before you leave!

Money

❐ **Bring a small quantity of bills in the local currency; bring other bills in US dollars.** Depending on the country, it might be a good idea to carry a couple hundred dollars in the local currency. For Costa Rica, I don't bother with this because US dollars are accepted and changed easily. But I do bring enough cash, like one or two thousand dollars. Some people might not feel comfortable bringing that much cash. But I'm okay with it, and I like having the cash ready.

Traveler's checks are usually more hassle and are not accepted everywhere. I personally no longer use them.

Instead, use a combination of cash, credit and debit cards.

❐ **Make sure your debit card works abroad, and inquire with your bank about the charge for using it.** They may have a plan to waive the fee.

❏ **Call credit card companies to advise you'll be away.** You need to advise your credit card company you'll be away before your trip. Otherwise, your credit card will probably be blocked when you attempt to use it in a foreign country.

❏ **Be set up for online banking.** If you're not set up already, do it now!

Pets

❏ Find someone to take care of your pets.

House or Apartment

❏ **Arrange for someone to take care of houseplants, and come by to check on the house.** I personally don't have houseplants, so that's solved right there. But I do have a family member regularly check on the place.

❏ **Lower heating to lowest safe level.** You will save a lot in heating bills just by leaving during the winter! But make sure you at least keep a safe temperature in the house.

❏ **Inform security alarm company** (if you have one).

❏ **Call house insurance company to notify you'll be away.**

❏ **Unplug electronics.** Actually: unplug everything except things your trusted friends will use when coming by. Electronics such as TVs and DVD players use up electricity just by being plugged in.

❏ **Don't change your message on your machine.** Don't leave a message such as "Hi. I'll be away for three months in the Dominican Republic," as some people do. Keep the same message on your machine.

☐ **Consider using a time-switch to turn on some lights at night.** Inquire at your hardware store. This will give the appearance of someone still living in the house.

Other Considerations

Should you advise your neighbors and landlord that you're leaving? This is a personal choice. Personally, I don't tell anybody except close friends and family members that I'm leaving. Plus, I never share my personal address publicly.

Packing

☐ **Verify weight requirements for your bags, and pack early.** Most airlines have a maximum amount you can bring in your checked luggage. In most cases, you can bring two bags of 50 lbs each. To make sure you don't go over that limit and have to pay extra, make sure to weigh your luggage in advance!

Appendix 3:
Checklist of Things to Bring...
That Are Not Easily Found in Paradise

Generally, people tend to bring MORE things than they really need when they leave for an extended period of time.

Now that the world has become a big "global village," it's become a lot easier to find almost everything, anywhere.

Planning on bringing **EVERYTHING** that you think you might need on your trip is often an unnecessary hassle. Most items can be found abroad.

Tim Ferriss, author of the book "The 4-Hour Workweek," recommends creating a "relocation fund" of around $300 to buy the things you might need when you move, so you don't have to burden yourself with more stuff than you need.

But even though it's possible to find almost anything you need abroad, there are a few items that can be harder to find .

So with this checklist, I'm going to show you what you probably should bring, what you probably should leave behind, and what you might or might not find abroad.

I'm also going to give you my personal checklist of things I bring when I leave.

Keep in mind: if you're going to relocate to an archipelago in the South Pacific, you definitely won't have access to a lot of items that can easily be found in Central America, Europe or Asia.

My New Philosophy

I used to bring much more than I do now. But I got a tip from experienced backpackers, who taught me to pack light.

For example: I was often afraid of missing certain items when I was away. I would bring a guitar and schlep it around, when in fact I wouldn't use it for months. Now, I have bought a guitar in Costa Rica that I use there. It was not expensive at all, and suits me well.

If you work online, I would also bring a small travel printer and a scanner (I recommend the Fujitsu ScanSnap S1100).

So the trick is to bring anything you can't live without and would have a hard time finding at your destination, and buy the rest there, using the "relocation" fund we talked about.

Checklist of Things to Bring

Essentials

You will want to bring your personal items and the necessary small essentials . Here's a short list:

❐ **Digital camera**

❐ **Battery for your camera**

❐ **Camcorder for recording video**

❐ **Your cellphone** (especially if it works internationally) r **A small notebook, with many pens**

❐ **Laptop computer**

❐ **A Flash drive for storing data**

❐ **iPod or music player, with headphones**

❐ **A good pair of running shoes**

❐ **Watch or travel alarm clock**

Clothes

In tropical countries, you generally need fewer clothes. But because of heat and humidity, I think you cannot bring too much underwear.

For a long trip, I recommend bringing the following, per person, and buying the rest onsite as needed:

❐ 5 T-shirts (I recommend the Icebreaker line, because they are made with merino wool, dry quickly, and don't smell.)

❐ One thin long-sleeved shirt (to protect against the sun)

❐ 3-4 pairs of shorts (include some quick-drying shorts and two pairs of "dressy" shorts)

❐ 1 pair of pants or jeans

❐ Lots of underwear!

❐ 5-6 pairs of socks

❐ 1 thin raincoat

❐ 1 hat

❐ 1-2 swimsuits

❏ Your favorite pair of sandals (those are easy to find, but if you have a pair you really like, bring them along)

You will want the long-sleeve + the raincoat in case it gets a little chilly or it rains at higher elevation. But don't bring too many warm clothes. You simply won't need them.

Everything else you might need can be bought onsite.

Kitchen Items

I personally bring my Vita-Mix blender on any long trip. Even though it's heavy, I use it so much, and it's very difficult to find abroad.

So if you're into health foods as I am, here's a quick list of things you might want to bring:

❏ A Vita-Mix or other heavy duty blender (don't bother bringing other types of blender. You can find those anywhere).

❏ Your best multi-purpose knife

❏ A foldable, flexible cutting board

❏ 1 tupperware-style plastic container

❏ 1 spoon, 1 fork (this is just for when you're on the road)

Personal Care

I only bring the following:

❏ A pack of razors (because I don't know what quality I will find when I arrive)

❏ 1 small bar of soap

❐ 1 toothbrush

❐ Dental floss (my favorite brand)

❐ Brush and comb

❐ 1 plastic drinking cup

Everything else can be bought onsite. So this is a list of things you DON'T need to bring:

- Towels
- Toilet paper
- Cosmetics
- Shampoo and conditioner
- Antiperspirant
- Tampons
- Washcloth

Condoms are easily found, but may not be the same quality you can get in your country. So if you think you will need them, bring them along.

Keep in mind: if you have a favorite type of organic, chemical-free shampoo or toothpaste, you should bring it with you, as you don't know what you're going to find at your destination!

Books

One thing that you will NOT easily find abroad is books, or at least the kinds of books you want to read. That's why it's worth bringing a few good books for the length of your trip.

Because I read at least one book per week on average, it would take too much space to bring all the books I want for my trip. So that's why I use the Amazon Kindle. It's really been a boon to be able to bring dozens of books without having to physically carry them with me.

So bring with you:

❏ A series of books you'd like to read on your trip. Don't think that you're going to read more than you currently read now. Estimate based on your current reading speed

❏ Consider using an eBook reader such as the Amazon Kindle

❏ Bring a travel guide, such as Lonely Planet (you can also now buy the PDF versions of Lonely Planet books directly from their site. Then you can load them onto your laptop or Kindle to save space. But in my experience, the printed versions of these books still works better)

❏ Bring a pocket dictionary or language book (or better yet, load it onto your laptop or iPod)

Documents

Make sure you bring with you original photocopies of:

❏ Your passport

❏ Driver's license

❏ Insurance card and contact information

❏ Credit and debit cards

I personally scan these and add them to the program Evernote (**www. evernote.com**) for easy access).

Various

The following is a list of things you might want to bring, as they come in handy.

❏ A few plastic bags (to use for trash while traveling). On site, you will want to buy MANY Ziploc-type bags. They can be very useful in the tropics to safeguard your items from rain and humidity.

❏ A photo of your home and family (or have that on your iPhone). Eventually, this always comes in useful in conversations with natives of the country you're visiting..

❏ A Flashlight. I could advise you to get this onsite, but it's so useful to have sometimes, and it's small enough to just throw in the bag. Bring a small one with a bright LED beam (I recommend the Fenix.)

❏ A couple of needles

❏ Electrical adapter (Depending on the country you go to, they might use a different system. Don't get caught not being able to plug in your laptop when you arrive!)

What you DON'T need to bring

You can purchase the following easily on site:

- Umbrella
- Over-the-counter medications (such as aspirin)
- Batteries
- Sunscreen
- Insect repellant

Health Foods

There's no such thing as a "health-food store" in most countries of the world, at least not in the sense that we North Americans and Europeans understand it.

Although I suggest adapting to the foods that are available locally, you might want to bring some of your favorite seasonings that are not easily available in the country.

If you're a health food enthusiast, some items you won't easily find overseas include:

❐ Seaweed products

❐ Specialty salts

❐ Organic herbs and spices

❐ Apple cider vinegar

❐ Dates

I would have a hard time coming up with a complete list because pretty much every health food item you're used to WON'T be available overseas. What you will find is plenty of produce.

But if you need that special seasoning you use daily, then you should bring it along with you.

Things that are easily found:

- Olive oil
- Organic or chemical-free shampoo (although it may not be your
- preferred brand)

- Essential oils (not in every country)

Other Things to Pack:

- 5 or 6, or more, organic, fruit and nut bars

When I travel, I always bring a few fruit and nut bars from the health-food store. These are meant for the trip or for times when I'm traveling in the country and no food is available. They come in handy.

Entertainment

If you stay for a while in a tropical Paradise, eventually you'll get bored and want to watch a good Hollywood movie.

Where can you find such movies?

In most countries, street vendors will sell you pirated copies of popular DVDs. In fact, this is so common that in Asia even the regular stores sometimes sell these pirated copies. They usually go for $1 or $2.

You can join a movie-rental store and rent movies for about $1 (often those are pirated copies as well).

You can download these movies to your computer legally, using iTunes ($3-5).

You can use applications such as BitTorrent to download these movies, or the latest episodes of the TV shows that you watch, to your computer (note: this is illegal).

You can watch movies on cable TV. The good thing is that most movies are not *dubbed* but subtitled. So you can even improve your language knowledge in the process!

If you subscribe to a service like Netflix, you won't be able to use it overseas (except if you go to certain countries like Mexico, where the service is available. However, even then, you will only get the local selection).

One way around this is to use a VPN (virtual private network). This is a software that you install on your computer that will relay your Internet connection through a server in the United States, thereby pretending that you are physically present in that country. You can download the program Hotspot Shield (**www.hotspotshield.com**) or HideMyAss (**www.hidemyass.com**). Hotspot Shield is free but there are ads. You have to pay for the version without ads.

Having a VPN is almost indispensable anyway. This is the only way you can protect your data when using public wireless Internet. Also, you will be able to use other streaming services, like Hulu, to watch TV shows.

Other Things That Are Not Easily Found Overseas

Like I said earlier, most of the things you need can now be found in major cities around the world. However it's mostly a matter of how easy it will be for you to find these things, and how much of a hassle it might be.

Generally, household items can be found everywhere.

Shampoo, Gillette razors and products, dental floss, toothbrushes, and clothes: all of these things are easily found.

Even computer items such as flash drives, blank CDs, etc., are easily found.

But the selection is not the same... so the general rule is: if there's anything you can't live without and is special to you, bring it along.

From my experience, here's a list of other things that are hard to find (including some previously mentioned):

- Books, your favorite magazines
- The latest electronic gadgets
- Health food store items
- Higher-than-average quality items, such as Chef's knives, high-quality running shoes, etc.
- Ink for your travel printer
- Certain specialty clothing items

Remember that if you're going to be spending a long time in Costa Rica, it's worth using the mail service Aeropost (**www.aeropost.com**) to order products online that you might need.

Appendix 4:
The Costa Rica Rolodex!

My top overall contact is Jacqui Monacell at:

Your Costa Rica Contact

www.yourcostaricacontact.com

gerencia@mitchellca.com

Jacqui offers welcome packages, residency services, "concierge" type services, buying a car, finding an apartment, and anything to make your life easier as a newcomer to Costa Rica.

Residency

For help with residency matters, contact:

Monique Azuola

mazuola@hotmail.com

Mobile: 8374-8493 (dial country code 506 if calling from outside Costa Rica)

Visa Requirements

www.costarica-embassy.org

Association of Residents of Costa Rica

www.arcr.net

tel: 506/2221-2053

This company offers help with residency matters and living in Costa Rica. Recommended.

Live in Costa Rica Tours

www.liveincostarica.com

Christopher Howard is the author of the oldest and most popular book on retiring to Costa Rica. He offers retirement tours several times a year.

Renting a Car

In San Jose, contact:

Rent a 4 x 4

http://www.renta4x4incostarica.com/

In San Isidro del General (Southern Zone), contact:

Brunca

2770-4953

Cell: 8829-2136

They have lower prices than other agencies in the area.

Attorney

To open a company, handle legal matters, and more, contact:

Bernardo van der Laat Llinás

P & D LAWYERS

E-mail: **bvanderlaat@pdlawyers.net www.pdlawyers.net**

Getting a Cellphone

Getting a cellphone in Costa Rica can be a little complicated. The best way to do it is to open a company, and get the cellphone through that. The company can also be used for other purposes, such as buying real estate. Contact:

www.yourcostaricacontact.com

gerencia@mitchellca.com

Communities/Organic Living

For a great community and resources on organic living, contact:

Eric Rivkin

.Founder of Viva La Raw charitable foundation and Jewel of the Sun (La Joya del Sol) raw food retreat in Costa Rica

emrivkin@gmail.com

www.vivalaraw.org

Newspapers

Some of these resources are printed, some are available online. Read them regularly to understand what's happening in Costa Rica.

Ticotimes

www.ticotimes.net

Costa Rica AM

www.amcostarica.com

Inside Costa Rica

www.insidecostarica.com

Nacion

www.nacion.com

Private Mail Services

Aeropost or Aerocasillas

506-208-4848

www.aeropost.com

NOTE: Other services exist but only aeropost is recommended.

Airlines for Local Flights

AeroBell

www.aerobell.com

Nature Air

www.natureair.com

Paradise Air

www.flywithparadise.com

Sansa Airlines

www.flyansa.com

Recommended Blogs/Websites

The Real Costa Rica

http://blog.therealcostarica.com/

Living Abroad in Costa Rica

www.livingabroadincostarica.com

The Yahoo Costa Rica Group

http://groups.yahoo.com/group/CostaRicaLiving

Recommended Books

The New Golden Door to Retirement and Living in Costa Rica

Christopher Howard ISBN:1-881233-65-0

Moon Living Abroad in Costa Rica

Erin Van Rheenen ISBN: 1-59880-007-8

Choose Costa Rica for Retirement

John Howells

ISBN: 978-0-7627-488-6

Your Costa Rica Contact Offering "Welcome Package"

Jacqui Monacell has been my MOST important contact in Costa Rica. She offers the following "Welcome Package," which includes these services:

Cellular phone, line and delivery to your home anywhere in Costa Rica

Corporation (SRL) ready immediately in your name

PO Box in Miami for mail forwarding to Costa Rica

Local bank account with HSBC, BAC or BNCR

Concierge service that allows access to all referrals and services their office provides

All legal documents necessary for these transactions, including powers of attorney, personeria juridicas, etc.

Her website is: **www.yourcostaricacontact.com**

In the interests of full disclosure, I am NOT paid any commission for referring clients to her as part of this program.

Since she has been my best contact in Costa Rica so far for settling in, getting help, and even buying a car (which is a service that she offers), I asked her if she offered any "package deals" for those wanting to get set up here.

Please contact her for more information.

Appendix 5: Fruits of Costa Rica!

The *Delicious Dozen*, a list of my twelve favorite fruit delicacies of Costa Rica:

The malay or water apple (*la malaya o manzana de agua*), a light and refreshing fruit with a high water content, tastes similar to pears.

Naranjilla, a relative of the tomato, considered the Costa Rican version of the kiwi, tastes similar—mostly acidic with a touch of sweet.

Passion fruit (*maracuya*), sweet smelling with an acidic flavor, passion fruit works well as a dressing in fruit salads or mixed with other fresh juices or smoothies.

Granadilla, related to passion fruit, tastes sweet (sometimes referred to as sweet passion fruit). The best way to enjoy this fruit: simply cut it in half, spoon out the seeds, and enjoy!

Guavas *(guayabas)*, very sweet and delicious, four varieties common in Costa Rica: the criolla, the Chinese, the strawberry (or rose) and the cas (also known as the Costa Rican guava). Most of the guavas sold have been picked from trees in the wild. Take care when eating guavas, as many have worms in them!

The cacao fruit, encased in a hard shell, has a sweet and flavorful pulp that surrounds the cacao seeds. The seeds, processed in order to make chocolate, taste bitter in their raw state (as bitter as aspirin).

Star apple (*caimito*), a fruit available during the dry season (December to April), has a sweet and mild-tasting pulp. Cut in half and enjoy, but avoid eating the pulp close to the skin or seeds as these areas contain a latex-like substance that will stick to your lips!

Sapodilla (*chico*), the fruit that tastes like brown sugar, considered one of the most energy dense fruits found in the tropics, together with other types of sapote.

Pineapple (*piña*), one of the most popular tropical fruits worldwide, grows in abundance in Costa Rica. Three types of pineapples grow here: the classic yellow pineapple (also called *dorada*), the *criolla* (a pineapple with white flesh), and a hybrid of the first two varieties. The pineapples here taste extra sweet and cost very little (about $1 US each). My personal favorite pineapple, the *criolla*, tastes like vanilla frosting!

Mamey sapote (*zapote*), a fruit that tastes like sweet potato or pumpkin pie, has orange flesh and a large seed (sometimes two or three) in the middle. When cut in half, it resembles an avocado. Has a similar energy density to the sapodilla, another type of sapote.

Mango (manga), a fruit loved by almost everyone, grows here in abundance! The mango season starts in March and lasts for several months. During the season they cost about 50 cents a pound. Mangos, however, cost nothing when picked from the many wild trees around Costa Rica!

Soursop (guanabana)—this fruit has a mild, almost bubblegum like flavor with a texture similar to cotton candy. The fruit, eaten in various ways, is typically enjoyed freshly cut or in smoothies and juices.

A list of other fruits grown in Costa Rica

Coconut—ahhhh, coconut, a fruit that almost everyone has enjoyed! In addition to eating the coconut meat, many here also drink the water of the young coconut, the *pipa*. Most *pipas* are green, although there are light brown ones. This water has a sweet flavor and is mineral-rich and quite refreshing! During World World II, coconut water was used for blood transfusions.

Bananas—another popular fruit worldwide. A popular banana grown here, the *criollo* variety, has a sweet flavor almost like a fruit smoothie! There are many other varieties of bananas grown here that have a much better flavor than the standard Cavendish variety found in supermarkets. Plantain, a type of banana, although generally eaten cooked in Costa Rica, can also be eaten raw when very ripe. A plantain is ripe when the skin turns completely black.

Avocado—the Haas variety, the most popular avocado worldwide, does not grow easily here. The Haas avocados sold here are imported. The locally grown *criollo* avocado has a flavor and texture similar to the Florida avocado.

Blackberry (*mora*)—There are certain types of blackberries that can grow at higher elevations in Costa Rica. Due to the heat, the berries perish quite easily. Consume or freeze as soon as possible.

Apples—Due to the diverse climatic conditions in Costa Rica, apples can be grown at higher elevations. The local apples, available only in February and March, have a slightly tart flavor.

Strawberry—Strawberries grown here are very sweet and delicious. Not as fragile as the blackberries, they still need to be consumed or frozen as soon as possible.

Star Fruit (*carambola*)—This tart and acidic fruit is either loved or hated by those who try it! The entire fruit is edible, skin and all.

Citrus Fruits—The citrus fruits here differ from those found in other parts of the world. The lemons and limes are sweeter, while the oranges and grapefruits are sour. There is one variety of orange, the *criolla*, that is sweet, but it's not as sweet as varieties of oranges grown in Florida and California. The *criolla* oranges are best suited for juicing.

Cashew (*maranon*)—Cashew nuts are a popular snack, but the cashew fruit is also edible. It has a very astringent flavor.

Lychee (*lichi*)—Remove the spiny skin, and then enjoy the white pulp surrounding the seed, which has a flavor similar to grapes. Very delicious!

Tamarind (*tamarindo*)—The pulp of this fruit is the edible portion. It has a tart taste, despite its high sugar content. There is a high concentration of tartaric acid in it that gives it the tart flavor.

Guabas (*ice cream bean or inga*)—a fruit often grown in coffee plantations to provide the shade for shade-grown coffees. The part surrounding the seeds when opened is edible. It tastes like cotton candy!

Sugar Cane—To enjoy sugarcane, simply chew on the sticks and suck the juice out! Fresh sugarcane is water rich as well as nutrient dense. It's only when the fresh sugarcane is refined that the sugar loses all its nutrients.

Appendix 6:
Buying Food in Costa Rica

Much like the USA, there are different ways to buy food in Costa Rica.

Supermarkets

The most "modern" way is to shop at an air-conditioned supermarket. Although the selection is great for many household items, the cost for produce and other foods is higher at the supermarket than anywhere else you can buy them.

But the advantage with the supermarket is that you'll find more imported items (such as berries and apples), as well as a better selection of vegetables.

There are many supermarket chains in Costa Rica, such as "MegaSuper." Strangely enough, a supermarket is called just a "super," and sometimes you'll see a smaller market called a "mini super."

At the Megasuper, you can get a card that gives you savings any time you buy. There are no charges for this card, and you can ask for it the next time you go. It's mostly an incentive to return to the same chain. I'm not sure the prices are that much lower with the card.

Automercado is another chain that features a more upscale selection with more imported products.

Produce Stands

You can also buy fruits and vegetables at small produce stands you'll find in a lot of places. Generally, the prices are lower and the quality is better than at the supermarket.

"Guys" On the Street

Costa Rica is very much a "free enterprise" society, and you'll often find people parking a pickup truck on the side of the road, selling mangoes or pineapples.

You might be sitting in traffic, when another guy will pop out of nowhere and offer you items such as:

Agua de Pipa. This is coconut water, generally sold in a plastic bag. It's fresh, and usually cold, and you simply poke a hole in the bag with your teeth and drink.

Mango con Limon. I was puzzled for a long time about these green mangoes that people sell everywhere. Turns out that they are sliced green mangoes, served with slices of lemon and a little bag of salt. People squeeze the lemon on top of the mango, and add in some salt. I've never tried them, because the thought of eating unripe mangoes flavored with salt really doesn't appeal to me at all. But now you know what this is!

Bottled water, Platano chips (like potato chips, but made with plantain bananas), and "gelatina," which are sorts of popsicles.

Central Market

Another common place to buy food in Costa Rica is the "Central Market" (*Mercado Central*). This is different than the "Farmers' Market" (*feria*).

Every sizable town has a central market in the middle of it. Once you've been to one of these markets, you'll know them all, because they look pretty much the same.

The markets are in an enclosed space, but there are no doors to get in. It's open air.

Although it looks chaotic and unkempt, these places are generally very clean. You'll find various "sodas" (small Tico-style restaurants), produce stands, "bazaars" (stores selling various items, from children's books to hammocks), medicinal herbs, and sundries.

The market is generally open from Monday to Saturday, and closed on Sundays and holidays.

The best one I have seen so far is the one in Heredia, north of San Jose, where I stayed for a week in 2005. There I found pretty much every single exotic fruit available in Costa Rica, every day of the week!

Produce Truck

Yet another way to buy produce is from the "fruit and vegetable truck." In many neighborhoods, and especially in small towns that are far from stores, there's usually a guy (it's always a guy) who comes once or twice a week with a truck filled with fruits and vegetables.

They sell directly to you, right in front of your door.

Usually, they'll only stop for their usual clients. So you can ask around if there is such a truck that comes in your neighborhood, and if so, when. Then you can make an arrangement for the truck to stop at your place.

Pulperias

In addition to all the stores mentioned above, you'll find plenty of smaller stores. Some are called "pulperias," and generally only sell a few selected items, such as bottled water, cigarettes, chips, aspirin, etc.

Slightly larger stores are often called "Abastecedors," which is a small "general store" where you'll find a bit of everything that you might have forgotten at the supermarket.

Ferias

Finally, my favorite way to shop for food in Costa Rica is the *feria*, which is the local farmers' market, where farmers and even local families come to sell their produce.

At the feria, you'll find mostly fruits and vegetables, but also raw milk (cow and goat), eggs, and often a wide selection of random items.

Usually, the feria happens once a week, sometimes on two consecutive days.

In Heredia, the farmers' market is on Saturday and Sunday.

In Alajuela, it's on Saturday (possibly Sunday as well).

In Perez Zeledon (San Isidro del General), it's Thursday and Friday.

Usually, if the feria happens over two days, you'll find the most variety and freshest produce on the first day, and then the lowest prices on the second day (as farmers are getting rid of anything they haven't sold).

The widest selection of food is to be found in the Central Valley. So far, my favorite farmers' market has been the Alajuela one. But I heard that the Heredia market is possibly even better.

The Alajuela market featured a mind-boggling selection of the freshest mangoes, papayas, soursops, pineapples, vegetables, and all the exotic Costa Rican fruits you can think of.

Certainly, an advantage of living in the Central Valley is this access you get to the best produce in the country.

The Perez Zeledon market is also nice, but doesn't feature nearly as many merchants.

If you're going to spend any time in Costa Rica, I highly encourage you to find out when is the next *feria* in your area. You don't want to miss that!

"Sodas"

The word "soda" in Costa Rica actually means: a small restaurant serving typical Costa Rican food.

These "sodas" are everywhere. The name comes from the free advertising banners given by Coca-Cola and other soft drink companies.

You can go in any of these establishments and mingle with the locals, and practice your Spanish by ordering a plate of Gallo Pinto (rice and beans) for breakfast, or a typical Costa Rican lunch. Most sodas are not open for dinner.

Foods to Try in Costa Rica

I've never seen a restaurant serving Costa Rican food outside of Costa Rica! That's probably because the cuisine is not known to be extraordinary. Most people say it's too bland or boring. However, that's probably because they haven't taken the time to try out what's really available.

On your next trip to Costa Rica, in addition to the local fruits, try some of these foods!

Gallo Pinto. Gallo pinto is the national dish of Costa Rica. It means "spotted rooster" due to its appearance, but most people just call it "pinto." It's essentially pre-cooked rice and black beans stir-fried with some onion, garlic and perhaps some other veggies. It's served for breakfast, but you can ask for it in most sodas at other times of the day. The Costa Rican version is not very healthy, using large amounts of oil and salt, so make sure to ask it to be made lower fat if that's important to you.

Casado. What do Ticos eat for lunch? Rice and beans, of course! The national lunch dish is called "casada." Here's what it consists of: half the plate will be rice, and then the rest will include: black beans, cabbage salad, a portion of meat, fish or chicken, and sometimes fried plantains or other vegetable dishes. It's often served with corn tortillas.

Patacones is a junk food served in many sodas and restaurants. It's green plantains fried and sprinkled with salt.

Cabbage Salad. This salad is served everywhere in Costa Rica. I have provided the recipe at the end of this book!

Picadillo. This is a vegetable dish made with finely diced vegetables, cooked with seasonings. It sometimes contains meat. The main vegetable used is often diced, green papayas, which are sold in bags in supermarkets. If you're wondering what this bag of white cubed veggies is, the mystery is solved!

Tortillas. Costa Ricans eat tortillas with most meals. They are made with corn only, and therefore are gluten free. I like to eat them with avocado, beans and salsa. They are similar to the tortillas Mexicans used for soft tacos.

Natilla. There's a strange type of sour cream sold everywhere in Costa Rica. It's not as sour as the American version, and also not as rich. People eat it with rice and beans!

Pejibaye. No trip to Costa Rica is complete without trying this "fruit" with a lot of history. The pejibaye grows on a palm tree. It's thick, fibrous and is the size of a big walnut. It's usually sold pre-cooked, and tastes like hard pumpkin or chestnut. Most Costa Ricans eat it with mayo! I enjoy it with guacamole. But the best way to eat pejibaye is in soup. It's delicious that way, as most of the grittiness of the fruit goes away. Pejibaye is essentially a carb, but also contains more fat than other carbohydrates like potato.

Chayote. This vegetable is botanically a fruit. It looks like a big green pear with an odd shape, and is served almost every day in Costa Rica. It's very mild and doesn't taste like much to most people. I like it, as it reminds me of summer squash or cucumber (and it is in the same family), but harder.

Yuca. This is a white, very starchy root vegetable that is used to make tapioca. In Costa Rica, you will find it served boiled or fried. There are also amazing chips made with it!

Drinks

Coffee. Coffee is popular in Costa Rica, but it's not as strong and caffeinated as American or European versions. A cup of coffee usually costs 50 cents in most sodas.

Chan. This is an interesting drink to try. It's made with fruit juice and chia seeds, called "chan" in Costa Rica, and sold in most supermarkets. The chia seeds swell up and become gelatinous in the drink. It sounds gross, but tastes fine, and the locals believe it's good for digestion.

Fresco de Tamarindo. This is the Costa Rican version of lemonade. It's made with the sour tamarind pods (a common tropical fruit), sugar, water and ice.

Beer. Ticos love beer. In fact, you'll see signs for the local brew, the Imperial, everywhere. Unfortunately, it's the most mediocre of the local beers, but revered by the locals. The Bavaria is a better local brand.

Wine. Wine drinking is not common in Costa Rica, but you can find imported wines in all upscale supermarkets.

A Few Costa Rican Recipes

Fat Free Raw Vegan Cabbage Slaw Costa Rican Style

Serves 4 as a side dish

Ingredients:

5 cups green cabbage, sliced (or slaw mix)
1 medium ripe tomato, diced
1/3 cup white onion, diced
1 -1 1/2 large limes, juiced
1/2 tsp salt
1/4 tsp fresh ground pepper or to taste

Directions:

1. Place cabbage or slaw mix into a bowl. Add tomatoes and onions and seasonings. Roughly squeeze and massage the cabbage to wilt it and make the tomatoes release their juices.
2. Taste test and add more lime or salt if desired.
3. Let sit in the fridge for at least 30 minutes to soften before serving.
4. Serve with raw entrees or as a topping for vegan tacos or rice and beans.

Variations:

You can also add some chopped raw cilantro (coriander) or parsley if desired. Julienned carrot or celery, red cabbage, or jicama can be used to mix it up as well.

Chan Drink

This drink is made with chia seeds, which are sold everywhere in Costa Rica under the name "chan."

- 2 Tbs of chia seeds ("chan")
- 5 cups of water
- Lemon or lime
- Honey (to taste)

Add the chia seeds to the water and brink to a boil. Let it boil for one minute. Remove from heat and let it set uncovered until it cools.

Blend this liquid with lemon or honey to taste. Usually one lemon and honey to taste will work. Chill in the fridge and serve.

I personally like to simply add the chia seeds to fruit juice and let it soak in the fridge overnight.

Fresco de Tamarindo

This other drink is easy to make. You will need:

- 4 cups of water
- ¼ of a pound of fresh tamarind
- Sugar or other sweetener to taste.

Tamarind is sold with the seeds. Take the tamarind and dilute it in a water pitcher, and let it soak for 24 hours. Add sugar or sweetener to taste, and strain to remove seeds. Serve very cold!

Gallo Pinto, the National Dish

Gallo Pinto (Rice and Beans)

The Costa Ricans generally make this traditional dish with a lot of cooking oil and beef bouillon cubes. I have modified it so that it is vegan and oil free.

Below you will also find separate recipes for cooking the rice, black beans and making tamarind sauce.

Serves 4-5

To make Gallo Pinto you need:

- 4 cups cooked white rice (cold and refrigerated)
- 4 cups, cooked black beans (about 2 15 oz. cans)
- 2 red bell peppers, deseeded and diced
- 1 large onion, diced
- 3 tsp. garlic, minced
- 1 cup cilantro, chopped (about 1 bunch)
- 2 tsp. better than bouillon vegetable seasoning or 1 bouillon cube
- 5 tbsp Tamarind sauce or 4-5 tbsp vegan Worcestershire sauce
- 1/2 tsp fresh ground pepper *optional
- 1/2 tsp Herbamare or salt *optional

Directions:

In a large wok, sauté onion, garlic and peppers in black bean juice (reserved or from can) for 6-8 minutes until slightly soft. Use vegetable broth if it dries out or more black bean juice.

Add black beans and seasonings and cook for another 5-6 minutes until the peppers are cooked to your liking. Be careful not to stir too roughly and break the beans.

Add the cold rice and gently stir to cover with black bean juice and spices. Do not over stir or you will break the ends and it will become mushy and sticky. Make sure there is just enough liquid to cook it and you don't have too much so that it's too wet, or too little that the rice is burning at the bottom.

Gallo Pinto Tamarind Sauce Recipe

- 1/2 cup water
- 1 tsp sugar
- 1 tsp dijon
- 2 tbsp tamarind (4 pods, peeled and deseeded)
- 1 tsp apple cider vinegar
- 1/4-1/2 tsp pepper
- 1/2 tsp herbamare or salt
- 1/4 tsp soy sauce
- 1/4 tsp celery seed
- 2 cloves of garlic

Combine ingredients in a Vitamix or high powered blender and blend until combined and tamarind is in smallish pieces. Be careful not to break your blender!

Strain tamarind fibres out with a fine mesh strainer or cheese cloth.

Use on gallo pinto or other bean dishes.

Rice Recipe:

Rice:

- 2 cups regular long grain regular white rice (not basmati or jasmine)
- 1 small bay leaf
- 1 tsp. Herbamare or salt

Directions:

Combine ingredients in a rice cooker and add almost enough water to the 2 cups fill line. Use a little less if you like firm rice.

If using the stove, see package directions for how much water to use and how long to cook. Use a little bit less water for firmer rice.

Cook your rice the day before or in the morning. Once it's done, let it steam 10-15 minutes and then immediately fluff with a fork. Take out and spread out on a tray and let it cool. Store in the fridge. This prevents it from getting mushy when reheated.

Black Beans Recipe:

- 1 cup uncooked dried black beans, or 2 cans of black beans
- 1 bay leaf
- 2 tsp better than bouillon vegetable seasoning

Directions:

If using dried beans, soak for 3-4 hours. Do not soak overnight, they will absorb too much water and split. Drain and rinse.

Cook beans in a pressure cooker with enough water to cover and 2 tsp better than bouillon vegetable seasoning or herbamare and a bay leaf. If you don't have a pressure cooker, cook beans and bay leaf over medium low heat for 1 1/2 to 2 hours until done. Add seasoning at the end, or beans will take longer to cook.

Now put your beans and the bean water on the stove in a pot and season.

Pejibaye Soup

This soup is rich and should not be eaten if you're on a diet, except once, as you must try this delicacy!

- 10-12 pejibayes
- 3 cups vegetable stock
- 3 cups coconut milk
- 1 onion chopped
- 3 cloves garlic chopped or pressed
- 1 red, yellow or green sweet pepper.
- salt and fresh ground black pepper to taste

Method:

Purchase pre-cooked pejibayes at the supermarket in Costa Rica.

Sauté the onion, garlic, and pepper in a pan with some vegetable stock until the onions are clear. Blend the pejibayes with the rest of the vegetable stock in a blender, and then combine all ingredients in a stockpot and simmer for another 5-10 minutes.

Final Words

I really hope you've enjoyed this book.

If you're curious about how I manage to make a living from anywhere in the world, please check out the other resources I have available on the subject.

I offer these two resources:

* My course *How to Make a Living in the Natural Health Movement* —The 10 modules in this course will give you all the tools you need to succeed in making passive income doing what you love in the natural health movement. For more information, go to: **www.fredericpatenaude.com/makealiving.html**

* My mentoring program *Do What You Love Success Group* — This is my ongoing program for making a living doing what you love. You'll love the resources, information and support I offer in it. Currently, the program offers:

Complete Training Program on How to Make a Living Online. As part of your subscription to the Do What You Love Success Group, you will also receive a complete training program covering many aspects of the making a living on the Internet.

You will get access to carefully designed special reports once every two weeks that will answer the many questions you probably still have about various aspects of making a living online.

These lessons really cover a lot of ground! I recommend taking time to go through them each week. You'll find them easily digestible and easy to put in practice.

You'll find that some of these reports cover basic elements, while others go into much more advanced technique. Overall, they'll give you a great education on the many aspects of running an online business.

Each report is in PDF format for easy reference and printing.

Topics include:

- How to drive massive amounts of traffic to your site
- How to automate your marketing, so you can spend most of your time doing what you love
- Detailed information on how to build your list using Internet ads
- How to start your own coaching program, making $1000 to $10,000 or more helping others one-on-one or in group situations
- How to create your own membership-type programs, for consistent monthly income
- And more!

For more information on the Success Group, go to:

www.dowhatyouloveuniversity.html/new.html

--

To receive my free newsletter on making a living doing what you love, go to:

www.dowhatyoulove.com

For my free newsletter on the topic of health and nutrition, go to:

www.fredericpatenaude.com

Your secret URL is:

www.fredericpatenaude.com/secretcostarica/

Made in the USA
Las Vegas, NV
24 August 2024